WOMEN DON'T OWE YOU PRETTY

Andrews McMeel Publishing
a division of Andrews McMeel Universal
1130 Walnut Street, Kansas City, Missouri 64106

www.andrewsmcmeel.com

22 23 24 25 26 SDB 10 9 8 7 6 5 4

ISBN: 978-1-5248-5756-1

Library of Congress Control Number: 2020941208

Editor: Allison Adler
Designer: Jaz Bahra
Art Director: Holly Swayne
Production Editor: Elizabeth A. Garcia
Production Manager: Carol Coe

Attention: Schools and Businesses
Andrews McMeel books are available at quantity
discounts with bulk purchase for educational, business,
or sales promotional use. For information, please
e-mail the Andrews McMeel Publishing Special Sales
Department: specialsales@amuniversal.com.

WOMEN DON'T OWE YOU PRETTY

FLORENCE GIVEN

Andrews McMeel
PUBLISHING®

CONTENTS

AN INTRODUCTION

"You don't owe prettiness to anyone. Not to your boyfriend/spouse/partner, not to your co-workers, especially not to random men on the street. You don't owe it to your mother, you don't owe it to your children, you don't owe it to civilization in general. Prettiness is not a rent you pay for occupying a space marked 'female.'"
—Erin McKean

This quote changed my life and inspired the title of this book.

Throughout feminist history, women have explored the idea of prettiness as a currency, and there are a lot of variations on this idea out there. For example, Naomi Wolf's book *The Beauty Myth* is a deep dive into how our beauty standards are linked to capitalism; Chidera Eggerue touches on prettiness in her book *What a Time to Be Alone*, and her #SaggyBoobsMatter movement promotes a message of anti-perfection; and trans activist Janet Mock has spoken about how she felt she gained pretty privilege when she began her transition. This book—*Women Don't Owe You Pretty*—is my interpretation.

This phrase sent me on a journey of unpacking my identity, forcing me to properly examine myself for the first time and ask why the hell I was performing these invasive, expensive, time-consuming, and, at times, painful beauty rituals. I realized how much of my self-worth was determined by whether or not I appeared desirable to men, and whether that desirability would be enough to encourage them to treat me with respect. But most of the time the attention that my "prettiness" garnered meant that men viewed me as an object, and men don't respect objects. After all, objects are something we use without reciprocity; it's a one-sided relationship. It's why they didn't handle my rejection well and called me "frigid"—because objects aren't supposed to have their own desires and motivations. They're objects. Acknowledging this was both uncomfortable and liberating—exactly what growth is supposed to feel like.

This phrase also forced me to examine the kinds of standards against which someone's "prettiness" is measured, and what "pretty" constitutes. In the Western world, our collective idea of what makes someone pretty is almost always based on their proximity to being white, cisgendered, thin, and nondisabled. This helped me to see how my own prettiness has given me opportunities—opportunities that women who fall outside of what society deems as pretty have to work harder for, or never get at all. Whether I thought I was attractive or not, for the first time I had to acknowledge the objective fact that I sit high on society's scale of desirability by being slim, nondisabled, and white. As women we don't want to admit that we have "pretty privilege" because we have been taught that we should be unaware of our beauty, and to respond to compliments with self-deprecation like, "No, I'm not, look at my . . . [points to 'flaws']!" In order to acknowledge that we have this privilege, we must first acknowledge that we are, in fact, pretty. Which, due to insecurity and our societal conditioning, is near impossible for most women. This is how our desirability privilege is silently maintained.

There's a discussion about whether desirability really is a privilege, since its benefits are rooted in the objectification of our bodies, not respecting our whole selves. My prettiness is both the thing that causes people to treat me better and also the thing that has led to the most traumatic experiences of my life. Men don't look at pretty women on the street and think, "She's pretty, so I won't sexually harass her or follow her home." It's the opposite. I walk through life with constant vigilance—anxious about the next man who'll stick his head out his car window and shout something at me, who'll spike the drink that my "prettiness" encouraged him to buy for me, or who'll force me to stop in a shop before I go home to make sure I'm not being followed. Keys between my fingers, heart racing, checking over my shoulder, strategizing my safest route home even if it means spending money on a taxi—this is what navigating public spaces looks like for a lot of women. I can't tell you the amount of times I have contemplated shaving my head to reduce sexual harassment. But to do so would be giving in to the idea that it's my responsibility to prevent this harassment, not theirs.

I was taught how to count calories, have boundaries with, and say "no" to food as a young girl, before I learned about the importance of having boundaries with and saying "no" to other people. What do you think that taught me about being a woman in this world? I learned that it was more important for me to be an object of desire than it was to have my own needs met and be respected as a person. These harmful belief systems and low self-esteem landed me in abusive relationships—my boundaries were nonexistent, and I didn't believe I deserved better. I was just happy that someone wanted me. I often wonder what my life would look like if I had learned that my body belongs to me, and me alone, first; that the way my body looks, and its purpose, is not to please others. I wonder what my life would look like if I had understood that I do not owe anybody "nice," "perfect," "petite," or "pretty"; that the best version of myself is not the one that is broken down in order to fit into the room afforded for women in a man's world but is the version that stays whole in spite of other people's reactions—whether there is space for me or not.

Instead, I squashed, minimized, and even killed parts of who I really was in favor of the validation I craved, living to please everyone but myself—and I don't want you to feel as though you have to do the same. This is the book I wish I could have whacked myself over the head with before the world's toxicity permeated my sense of self.

Here's what a conversation between my younger self and older self would have sounded like.

Older Floss: Floss, why are you stuffing your bra and skipping breakfast?

Younger Floss: Because that's what boys like! Skinny girls with big tits.

OF: Okay, Floss, can I have a word?

YF: Yeah, what's the problem?

OF: Well, what you do with your body is your choice and your choice only. But I think it's really important for you to understand that what you're doing to yourself is actually very unhealthy. Can you tell me why you're skipping meals?

YF: Because "nothing tastes as good as skinny feels"! I'm not doing it for men. I just like the way it looks.

OF: Jesus. Okay. First of all, I know you're in 2013 right now, but it's 2020 where I am, and Kate Moss herself has since publicly regretted ever saying that. Your weight does not define you and it is not a measure of your beauty; that concept is now OBSOLETE. Second of all, the reason you want to do this to yourself may not be consciously motivated by wanting to attract men. However, our collective idea as a society of what is "pretty" and "desirable" is informed entirely by racism, sexism, fatphobia, disablism, transphobia, and male desire. Do you notice how boys just show up to school with scruffy hair and sleep in their eyes?

YF: But it's just different for bo . . . Oh. I see. Yeah, I guess that's not fair, is it?

OF: No, it isn't. While the boys get to wake up ten minutes before school starts, you spend an entire morning looking in the mirror making yourself up, skipping your breakfast in an attempt to be a slim, pretty object of their affection. I know you're exhausted. Have you ever thought about what you could do with that extra time? Have you ever wondered what your life might look like if you just showed up as you are?

YF: Wow, I hadn't thought of it like that. I guess it would be easier if I could just roll out of bed and turn up . . . but still, it's normal to want to be pretty!

OF: And why do you feel so strongly that men need to desire you? Do you believe a woman's worth is tied up in her ability to be pretty?

YF: I never thought about it like that. I guess maybe I do . . .

OF: So, if you feel that way, and you believe that your worth as a woman is tied up in your beauty, how do you feel about women who aren't pretty? Do you look down on them? Do you think they're worthless?

YF: I don't think I do.

OF: Do you make yourself look this way because you like it, or are you performing femininity out of routine so you can be treated better by other people? The same way you know deep down that you yourself are nicer to women who perform femininity?

YF: OH MY GOD, STOP ATTACKING ME!

OF: It wasn't an attack, Floss. These questions are a mirror. Reflect on it and answer my question!

YF: Well, if I don't go to school with makeup on and my hair looking nice, people always mention it; they say I look tired. I get what you're saying. It's not fair and men get to just show up as they are blah blah blah. But if I look pretty, people treat me way better—boys treat me way better!

OF: Why do you feel the need to be chosen by men? Why can't you just go to school to learn?

YF: I . . . don't actually know. Again, it's what I've always been told I should want—a man, that is. I guess I never thought to ask myself why I want to be "chosen by men," or where that came from.

OF: If you have to perform a level of "prettiness" in order to be chosen by someone, they are choosing you based on your beauty. I know that you want to be chosen for your entire self. Darling, as long as you spend your time chasing male validation, you will exhaust yourself all the way to your grave. Because male validation is a bottomless pit. It won't ever see you how you deserve to be seen. Stop chasing it. Stop trying to attract it. Stop trying to mold yourself into a palatable Floss. It will consume you and spit you back out. Your main goal in life is not to be "chosen" by a man anyway. It's all a big lie. You don't actually need men for anything. Or at the very least, not in the capacity you've been made to think you do.

YF: What about money? I've always thought I'd marry a rich man . . .

OF: If that's what you want to do, that's fine. But also, go make your own money first. Be your own rich man.

YF: Fine—what about having kids?

OF: Do you even want kids? Or do you feel a pressure to have them because, as well as her ability to be beautiful, a woman's worth in this society has also been based on her ability to reproduce? You are not a failure if you do not have children . . .

YF: Jesus—not have children? I'll get back to you on that one. What about for sex and love? We need men for sex!

OF: Buy a vibrator. Also, contrary to the messaging of the media you have been consuming your entire life, men aren't the only option for a potential romantic partner! Have you ever considered that you might be attracted to other genders?

YF: Well, shit.

OF: Mm-hmm . . .

YF: I've always wanted to date women and people of other genders, but I'm attracted to men too, so I figured my feelings for other people were invalid . . .

OF: You see?! We are taught in so many ways that we need to rely on men to be happy. But you don't. And by the way, hun, you're queer as hell.

YF: So, what you're saying is that I only require men to be in my life in a capacity that adds to my already amazing existence?

OF: YES . . .

YF: I don't have to compromise myself because . . . I'm enough on my own?

OF: YES! Encouraging women to spend hours focusing on their prettiness and desirability for men, instead of directing that energy towards themselves, means that men keep making all the money, having all the fun, while women are expected to compete for their attention and are shamed for doing the exact same things they do.

YF: Why would women be shamed for doing the same things as men? That doesn't seem fair.

OF: You're right—it isn't. But when women choose to behave outside of our appointed, prescribed gender roles, it unravels centuries of oppressive structures and some people can't handle being challenged like that. In the name of preserving this "tradition" they use shame to keep us in our place. And it's not even always men who police us. When we turn against each other, it's patriarchy's very sneaky way of continuing our oppression—it gets other women to do its dirty work.

YF: But what's the point in "being myself" if that version of me is going to be treated poorly and criticized? Why don't I just carry on the way I am, performing femininity for men, and doing what's expected of me, so the world continues to reward me?

OF: Points well made. I hear your confusion, and that's a very important and valid question. Performing femininity and prettiness for a lot of women is survival. You're right. Why would you take the difficult route of Being Yourself when you know that there's a much easier, well-traveled path you can take instead? One where you are treated better, and all you have to do is grab a makeup brush and a razor!

YF: That's what I mean!

OF: It's true that society rewards women who don't have to be told to stay in their lane. It loves women who just readily accept their gender roles and conform. Doing little things to please men will afford you a lot of advantages. However, femininity can also be the thing that people mistreat us for. You need to look no further than a man's reaction to someone who just told him he's "acting like a girl" to see how true this is. If one of the worst things you can call a man is "a girl," what does that mean he thinks about girls?

YF: Wow. I guess that explains why I pride myself so much on being "not like the other girls."

OF: Exactly, and the "other girls" are all of us. Cut that shit out! This is called internalized misogyny: you are trying to distance yourself from femininity as much as possible, to win over the attention of men.

YF: Okay, I think I get it. What you're saying is that, either way, no matter what I do as a woman, I can't win? There's always going to be compromise?

OF: Yes.

YF: That sucks.

OF: Not if you change your perspective.

YF: How do you mean?

OF: Well, if you're going to be punished either way, tell me, what option does that leave you with?

YF: To do whatever the fuck I want?

OF: Exactly.

CHAPTER 1

FEMINISM IS GOING TO RUIN YOUR LIFE

(IN THE BEST WAY POSSIBLE)

"The truth will set you free, but first it will piss you off."
—Gloria Steinem

My journey into feminism was exhausting.

I lost friends, cried in nightclub bathrooms because the normalization of groping repulsed me to my core, screamed in the faces of men who catcalled me, and fell out with my parents on multiple occasions.

Very on-brand for me.

Very dramatic.

But I had to do this in order to grow. I had to (and still do, regularly) go through periods of sitting in toxic bullshit, abandoning old versions of myself, shedding skins, and experiencing uncomfortable transitions to be the person I am today—feeling confident enough in myself and my voice to write this book, speak my mind, and vocalize my experiences.

Growth can feel isolating. Everything you thought you knew about yourself and the world shifts right before your eyes. You'll start to notice unhealthy and toxic qualities in your friends as well as yourself. You'll stop enjoying your once-favorite movies when you realize they portray women as nothing more than a feast for male eyes and desires. The lyrics to your favorite Rolling Stones song will start to ring a little problematic, and you'll be disgusted to discover that sexism, racism, ableism, and transphobia exist almost everywhere, including the depths of your own subconscious mind. A shift in perspective has the power to flip the world as you know it upside down. But wouldn't you rather see the world clearly than walk through life oblivious to all that you are complicit in and enabling?

Don't be a passenger in your own life.

Having your world turned upside down and experiencing temporary discomfort is minor in comparison with the suffering you would have endured and inflicted onto others over the course of your life if you had left these things unchecked. *Temporary discomfort is an investment in your future self.* Accept a small and uncomfortable transition now for a lifetime of potential growth and self-development. Feminism and self-discovery will uproot your entire life, but it's going to be worth it. I promise.

YOU WON'T BE ABLE TO ENJOY THINGS ANYMORE
Enter feminism, the world of hating everything.

Just kidding! *Kind of.*

But, baby, once those goggles are off, there's no going back. You're going to see the misogyny, racism, and double standards in absolutely *everything*:

- One minute "chick flicks" are your favorite movies, the next they're the stereotype-perpetuating garbage that you blame for making you crave male validation.
- As you learn to understand consent more clearly, past sexual experiences that left you feeling uncomfortable might now actually be reconsidered as assault or rape.
- Yes, you'll find yourself enraged over the slightest things. Right down to how much space men take up on public transportation with their legs and how you instinctively cross yours.
- Yes, you might realize how your own behavior changes when you interact with men, as well as your innate urge to be polite, desirable, and palatable.
- And yes, your eyes are going to open up to the fuckery in our society and your *own* poor behavior that has been so normalized. You might feel repulsed at yourself for never spotting it in the first place.

But guilt is an unproductive emotion. Feeling guilty for past mistakes and behaviors does nothing for you or the people you may have harmed unless it is accompanied by changed behavior. What matters is that you're aware now; you're waking up. And the actions you take moving forward are how you stop perpetuating further harm.

YOU WILL LOSE FRIENDS

With growth comes discomfort; this is inevitable. You have to be willing to potentially outgrow your peers, your friends, and even your family, if you're going to live a fulfilled life on your own terms, break cycles, and forge a new path. Hopefully, they'll grow with you or support you through your journey. But worrying about what others think when you're growing can't be your priority. Right now, just focus on *growing*.

This is probably the toughest thing you will face as you become more socially and politically self-aware. As you outgrow certain people in your life and embark on your journey of self-development, you'll see sides of them that you never did before. You might even feel guilty for outgrowing them and believe them when they tell you that you've "taken it too far" or that you're being "too sensitive." But remember that anyone who tells you you're "too" *anything* is using the word because they are threatened by your capacity to grow, evolve, and express your emotions. They want you to stay down there, with them—emotionally and morally stunted. You are a mirror reflecting back to them the parts of themselves that they know they're lacking.

While this might explain their behavior, it does not excuse it. People who are emotionally secure and have a strong sense of self won't feel intimidated by your need to express the emotional responses you feel. Those who do are lacking, and you are abundant. Never apologize for this. Being empathic and able to truly *feel* intensely is a gift, a talent, and something that people strive for.

You do not have to shrink yourself down to make others feel better about themselves.

Stop surrounding yourself with people who make you question your worth, and fill your life instead with people who choose to remind you of it—while simultaneously holding you accountable when you mess up. *Both of these things are acts of love.*

If I listened to every person who told me I've "taken my feminism too far" or believed every person who told me "not everything's about race/gender/sexuality," I'd still be stuck in ignorance and complacency. I'd be *exactly* the type of person the racist patriarchy relies on to keep these systems of oppression alive and thriving. Don't leave conversations about politics to "the grown-ups." *That's what the grown-ups want.* Patriarchy hates progressive conversations and disruptive people because it's a parasite that feeds on *silence and fear.* This is why the #MeToo movement founded by Tarana Burke has been so instrumental in raising awareness and challenging the normalization of sexual assault. When people shut you down for "speaking up," it's because they want the status quo to be maintained. It's a tactic as old as time. Stay headstrong. Keep going.

Most people don't want to acknowledge that most of what they think they know is false. *Who would?* Of course we're going to be reluctant to believe narratives that challenge our whole identity. It means realizing that we have been acting out of ignorance and through our subconscious minds our whole lives. Acknowledging this truth is uncomfortable. Knowing you have been unintentionally causing harm and benefitting from unfair systems is uncomfortable. But think about how uncomfortable it must be existing on the flip side of that privilege.

Imagine your identity as a woven piece of fabric—threads upon threads make up the unique person you are, just like your DNA: who you were told to be, who you were told to trust, how you were taught to give and receive love, and how you respond to certain situations. All of these factors make up your reality as you know it. Now imagine someone coming along and revealing something that challenges and unravels those threads and how that might make you feel. This is where people can become defensive. Rewiring our toxic and self-destructive patterns isn't supposed to be comfortable, but the more open-minded and aware you are to the fact that we all perceive and live *different* realities because our fabrics have been woven differently, the easier it becomes to grow, empathize, evolve (and reweave your fabric) with ease and self-awareness.

WORRYING ABOUT
WHAT OTHERS
THINK WHEN
YOU'RE
GROWING
ISN'T YOUR
PRIORITY.

JUST
GROW.

STOP JUDGING PEOPLE SO HARSHLY FOR THINGS YOU RECENTLY STOPPED DOING YOURSELF

I want to make it clear that people who are on the receiving end of abuse, whether directly from an individual person or by a system of oppression like racism, don't owe anyone their forgiveness. Rape survivors don't owe their rapist "second chances" because "people make mistakes." People of color do not owe white people forgiveness. Women do not owe men forgiveness. No one owes their abuser/oppressor *shit*.

I'm talking here about slipups that we ourselves make, or that others make in their journey to become more enlightened. Sometimes to cope with the realization that we have perpetuated toxic behaviors and tendencies, we find ourselves taking it out on others to assuage the guilt we feel about our newly discovered shortcomings. For example, it's only recently that I've come to learn how loaded the term "bitch" is when used as an insult. Once I realized how often I'd used this to describe women (who were often just assertive and reminded me of my own lack of boundaries and inability to say "no"), I'd jump down the throat of anyone around me who used the term "bitch," instead of just educating them the way that I was once educated.

Everyone should be held accountable for their actions, but we still need to extend the same forgiveness and room to grow that was afforded to us when we were still learning. Which, by the way, we still are. Every one of us—every day.

It's important to acknowledge red flags and abusive behaviors before they become a bigger problem, but people make mistakes. Do you have a friend who's really bad at communicating? Tell them. Does your mom make outdated comments about women's bodies? Does your grandma say racist shit? Do your friends shame other women for casual sex? Does your boyfriend insist on doing all the "man things" and making jokes about women in the kitchen (just dump him)?

Do you know white girls who wear cornrows while calling them "boxer braids" and sing *that* word in rap songs? Do you have a feminist BFF who "doesn't agree" with sex workers? Call them out. Inform them. *They* are the ones who should feel the pressure to change.

If you have the capacity, you can explain *why*, as white people, we can't say *that* word (yes, even though Kanye sings it) and *how* jokes about "women in the kitchen" perpetuate sexism. Explain to your mom the standards women's bodies are held to in comparison with men's; how we are expected to show up a certain way in this world; and ask, "Who are we to blame people for conforming under systems of oppression?" Remind your grandma that this isn't the 1960s, and you can't say shit like that anymore. In fact, that shit was never okay. Tell your BFF that sex workers are *not* the enemy of progress, that they are, in fact, exploiting the system built to oppress them and that is iconic as fuck (and, really, we should be taking notes).

It's a different story when someone is repeatedly causing harm. Some people just don't want to change. But you can still be a no-bullshit-taking, zero-tolerance person when it comes to sexist, racist, transphobic, disablist, homophobic garbage, while also allowing room for people to prove to you that they can grow, learn from mistakes, and bounce back with changed behavior—*just like you did.*

It's difficult when someone you love is saying something wrong and you don't want to correct them in case you come off as too "political" or "sensitive." But these are *exactly* the discussions you need to be having in order to change the world. Some people go their entire lives without ever questioning their identity, attempting to deconstruct patterns, or end cycles of inherited trauma, because they're too focused on *surviving*. It's easier to live by the narrative that has been supplied since birth because they don't have time to think about evolving. Having time to unpack and evaluate is in itself a privilege!

Having access to the internet, where so many diverse perspectives and marginalized voices have the ability to be amplified, is also an enormous privilege. So be careful to remember that not everyone has the capacity, time, and resources available to embark on this journey. It's important to share these resources when we have access to them, and call people in, not just call them out, when we can.

This journey is going to be long and hard.

It will tie knots in your stomach as you visit the dark corners of your mind and discover you've held lifelong beliefs about yourself and other people you weren't even aware of. Whenever I have a self-discovery breakthrough, I break *out*. Literally. My skin breaks out in zits—but I think those zits are beautiful. Each one of them represents my toxic behaviors, trauma, unhealthy coping mechanisms, and damaging beliefs surfacing after *long* processing, ready to exit my body. It's a sign that I'm shedding another skin, preparing for my glow-up. Then off we go again . . .

Feminism is going to ruin your life, but in the best way.

No more watching your subconscious drive your life around for you while you sit in the passenger seat. You're going to take the wheel and drive it your damn self. Because silence and complacency in situations of injustice make you complicit in the violence.

Speak up.

Say something.

FEELING GUILTY FOR PAST MISTAKES AND BEHAVIORS DOES NOTHING FOR YOU OR THE PEOPLE YOU HARMED, UNLESS YOU USE IT TO CHANGE YOUR BEHAVIOR.

CHAPTER 2

WOMEN DON'T OWE YOU PRETTY. BUT...

We live in a patriarchal society that prioritizes our desirability above anything and everything else.

Which means that . . .

Life is easier when we dress up.

Life is easier when we shave.

Life is easier when we wear makeup to work.

Life is easier when we have made a visible "effort" with our appearance.

Life is easier when we reflect society's idea of beauty. Full stop.

We are expected to show up and perform to expectations in order to be seen, and we know how to make our life easier if we apply the rules the patriarchy has set out for us. Look at where marginalized identities intersect with being a woman: trans women are still expected by society at large to perform this type of femininity to pass as a "real woman" (there's no such thing), and women of color are expected by society to perform "prettiness" to a further degree, in a world where whiteness has been positioned as the epitome of beauty. Historically there has been little representation of marginalized identities in the media, and even when there is, it's often a stereotypical, harmful portrayal, constructing these identities as inferior to the default of whiteness, thinness, and heterosexuality.

DESIRABILITY POLITICS—AKA "PRETTY PRIVILEGE"

Shaming other women for caring about their appearance is just another form of internalized misogyny and an inability to see how race, class, sexuality, and desirability all affect the way we're perceived in the world. In a world that prioritizes looks over everything else in women and affords you undeserved privileges once you reflect its ideal standards of beauty, how can we judge people who pay to do so?

It would be wonderful if women didn't feel the need to go to extreme measures to jockey for position in society's desirability hierarchy, but we cannot shame people for using the tools around them to make their lives easier. Whether that's a makeup brush or a razor, why would you want someone to suffer even more under the guise of having "superior feminist morals," when they're just trying to survive? We can't shame people for doing what they can to be seen and heard in this messed-up world.

Different women experience different levels of expectation from society to perform femininity. Marginalized women such as trans women, fat women, and women of color don't always have the privilege of "rejecting beauty standards" like growing out their armpit hair or even wearing their hair as it naturally grows on their head. Because of our racist and fatphobic beauty standards—which subconsciously enforce our "preferences" when dating, hiring people, and choosing friends—the way they simply exist in their natural state is seen as "undesirable" and they are treated as "less than" already, before even thinking about actively rebelling against gender norms.

Performing femininity and desirability isn't always a choice for marginalized women—it's often an act of survival.

Have you ever thought about how differently you would experience the world if your appearance changed? If you cut off all your hair, if you stopped wearing makeup—would it make you feel invisible? *Or maybe you have already experienced this!* Think about your own privileges within these preset standards of desirability and consider how they might have afforded you unearned benefits.

SHAVING

I stopped shaving my body the second I realized doing so had nothing to do with my own discomfort but was, in fact, entirely due to patriarchal brainwashing that led me to believe that my body hair was unattractive. I was fed up with being told that I should be repulsed by something that was part of my own body. I wanted to love my body, not hate her, and as a survivor of sexual assault, growing out my hair was a subtle and personal act of resistance and self-care that was instrumental to my healing process. It restored some of my autonomy, deciding that men and capitalism had no control over my body hair. *Fuck your overpriced pink razors. I'm gonna be a hairy bitch now!*

Growing out my armpit hair was a very intentional and conscious decision, but being able to grow out my body hair was, in fact, a privilege.

LIFE IS TOO SHORT NOT TO LOVE THE SHIT OUT OF YOURSELF.

Sure, it's not viewed as desirable by the standards of the male gaze—most people still think it's repulsive, and you will be shamed for it regardless of your race. But being able to grow out your body hair without facing *additional* discrimination is a privilege afforded only to thin, cisgender white women like me. Because even with my armpit hair (which I can shave off anytime I want) I will still be viewed as "desirable."

The ability to defiantly resist is only afforded to those who are already privileged enough not to be ostracized if they do so.

I don't know many trans women who grow out their leg or armpit hair, because they are held by society to much higher standards of "proving" their gender than cisgender women like myself are. Trans women and women of color don't owe it to anyone to perform their gender in a way that is hyper-feminine—but we live in a society that expects them to nonetheless. There are double standards associated with our acceptance of body hair that cannot be ignored, and conversations around hair positivity need to center the voices of those whose bodies are most marginalized by society's expectations in the first place. It does not make you morally superior to grow out your body hair and you're not any less of a feminist for shaving. Because let's face it, *life is easier when we shave.* Do what you want with your body hair! But remember that real change doesn't start until the people in the margins of our society are liberated and able to make the same decisions (without discrimination) that thin, nondisabled, cisgender white people can already make.

RE-BRAINWASH YOURSELF!

To begin unpacking your own desirability bias and "preferences," you can start by listening to, learning from, and respecting people you're not attracted to. If the content you consume is exclusively delivered to you by people you find palatable enough, thin enough, white enough, "nice" enough to listen to (me, for example, maybe?)—then I'm going ask you to level up and challenge your *bland taste buds*. If you're only willing to hear one side of any argument, then you are fundamentally limiting your scope and ability to see beyond your own viewpoint.

Work on diversifying the content you consume. If you're constantly accessing the same media delivered by the same people, how are you ever going to open your mind to other people's perspectives?

Unfortunately, straight white men dominate our media, and the media is our cultural storyteller.

Mass media is what shapes our culture, so we have to make a conscious effort to break out of its grip—it doesn't just happen. Take action now. Read books by Black folks. Follow fat, disabled, and trans people on Instagram. Seek out queer love stories. Listen to podcasts created by people of color.

Up until now we have been bombarded with the same stories that either make us subconsciously hate ourselves or hate others. It's time to change the narrative, and the power lies in your hands. Consume diverse content. Reinvigorate those tired taste buds.

AS A WOMAN
IN THIS WORLD, IT
OFTEN FEELS AS THOUGH
WE HAVE TWO CHOICES:

WE CAN EITHER BE
DESIRED OR RESPECTED.
SEEN OR HEARD.

WE RARELY EVER GET
TO EXPERIENCE BOTH
AT THE SAME TIME.
WHICH ONE WE EXPERIENCE,
OF COURSE, DEPENDS
ENTIRELY ON OUR
APPEARANCE.

CHAPTER 3

YOU ARE THE LOVE OF YOUR OWN LIFE

One of the most radical acts under capitalism is to simply love yourself. Especially if the love you have cultivated for yourself is enough to fill you, without the need for romantic love to feel validated.

I often think how much the younger version of myself would have hated the person I am today. If the 14-year-old me had heard me saying the words "I am the love of my own life," I would have thought of myself as conceited, self-obsessed, selfish.

In fact, dear reader, you might be doing the very same right now.

The truth is that, for a lot of people, it can be extremely uncomfortable to say nice, positive things about ourselves. For women in particular, we're taught that this makes us "vain." So when we hear others exude confidence, it can remind us that we don't really value ourselves as highly as we should. We're forced to see the reality that deep down we don't really love ourselves, and to cope we might try to tear down the people who do. But if we work on the relationship we have with ourselves, we can stop projecting our hurt onto others.

We live in a world that profits from our insecurities. Deciding that you deserve better is radical as hell, because you are actively going against centuries of social brainwashing and oppression; you are telling the world that you see through its bullshit.

**A new person is born in the moment you
say to yourself, "I deserve better."**

LIFE IS TOO SHORT NOT TO LOVE THE SHIT OUT OF YOURSELF

Most of the time, "self-love" and "self-care" are sold in a way that just further perpetuates the need for women to be constantly desirable and palatable. Treat yourself! Buy this face mask! Moisturize! We're not trying to sell you anything—this is about you! It's self-care! I don't know about you, but years of internalizing the messages about how women's bodies should look and the rigorous standards they're held to made me feel as though my body didn't belong to me. This kind of "self-love" takes me right back to square one: valuing myself based on the desirability of my face and body. While making myself up and feeling cute does bring me joy, it's only a temporary fix. It's instant short-term validation. It's a distraction.

I haven't learned to love myself through spa treatments or beauty products. Oh no. In fact, the journey started when, at fourteen, I lay in the middle of the busy park that all the girls from my school frequented and tried my hardest not to give a shit what any of them thought of me. I told myself that if I could lie there in the sun and listen to one song without caring what anyone thought, I could do literally anything. To make myself vulnerable and lay out in that park scared me, but it also unshackled me from living a life restricted by other people's perceptions. It was emancipating. I entered a world where I could do what brought me joy without caring about other people's opinions of why I did it. I stepped out of my comfort zone and got a taste of what my life could look like if I truly renounced the need to be liked.

Think about something you wish you could do. What is it that's stopping you from pursuing it? Do you hate the thought of being alone in public, or do you hate the perception you imagine other people have about you being alone? It sure was the latter for me. The idea of being out on my own? Bliss. The idea of people seeing me out on my own? Hell.

The truth is that no one is ever looking at you and thinking, "What the hell are they doing on their own?" If you've never done it before, promise me you will take yourself on a date. Don't take your laptop, don't use your phone; go completely and entirely alone with no other purpose than to simply eat, drink, and watch the world go by. Life is far too short to be waiting around for someone to ask you. You are the love of your own life, so act accordingly and take your damn self out.

PATRIARCHY WANTS YOU TO SETTLE. DON'T.

As a society, we have such an odd way of viewing single women. The way we talk to women approaching their thirties is often as though, if they don't couple up, they might actually combust. We pressure them to act while they're "still young and beautiful." Patriarchy has truly fucked up so many of us, to the point where we would rather be in a toxic relationship than have no relationship at all. Patriarchy wants women to settle.

I changed the way I viewed being single when I flipped my perspective. I realized it was a choice. By not settling and deciding to stay single, you have set your standards and you're sticking to them. You have decided that you deserve quality treatment (whatever that means to you) and anything that does not seek to add value to your life doesn't deserve a place in it. Simple!

"Single" doesn't mean "waiting for someone."

Choosing to be single is an autonomous choice, and a lot of men fear autonomous women and gender-nonconforming people. It reminds them that we have other purposes on this planet than to serve them. Women who don't have kids are called "selfish" and made to feel that their life is a waste. Women in heterosexual relationships who earn more than their partners are labeled "aggressive" or "bossy." Women who reject sexual advances are called "frigid," yet that same accuser would likely call a woman who enjoys casual sex a "slut." When people make autonomous decisions about their bodies and their lifestyles, they are met with a whole spectrum of resistance, and this is particularly true for marginalized people. Anything that deviates from the narrative society has written for and about you is shamed and unaccepted.

In a society that punishes you either way, the only option is to do what makes you happy.

Do you prioritize your romantic life over your own mental health, friendships, and the relationship you have with yourself?

If you could stop worrying about romantic love altogether, what would you be able to achieve with this new, enormous resource of energy?

STOP SETTLING FOR CRUMBS; YOU DESERVE THE WHOLE DAMN CAKE.

What are crumbs, you ask?

Crumbs are the *audaciously* small tokens and gestures that people throw us, in order to keep us under the illusion that they deserve a place in our lives—despite bringing very little (or no) value to it. We often allow this kind of behavior because low self-esteem leads us to believe that this is the kind of love we deserve, and over time it becomes normalized. Crumbs can be any of the following:

- Text messages
- Liking your Instagram pictures
- Replying/reacting to your Instagram stories
- Hitting you up randomly with a "wyd" text
- Complimenting you out of the blue, saying things they know will fluff your ego
- Dropping back in after a period of ghosting (when they're running low on self-esteem, you're their "hit" to make themselves feel better)

You'll notice most of the "interactions" listed occur online. That's because someone who gives you crumbs doesn't have any actual time for you IRL. Because, surprise! They don't value you. It's hard to hear, I know, but they value only what you can do for their own ego. If they do "make time" for you, you can bet it will always be when it suits them.

The *moment* someone shows the audacity of trying to keep you around for an exchange of crumbs, communicate to them that you want the whole cake (that you want to be taken out on a proper date or build a relationship or whatever that means to you). If they say they can't give it to you, that they're not ready to give you the cake, or they promise they can give you the cake at a later date, leave them where they are and move the hell on.

Make a promise to yourself to stop investing in people's potential. You're not a start-up investor.

When you settle for crumbs, it sends a message that that's all you think you deserve. Users know that they can get away with doing the absolute bare minimum to have a seat at your table. That they can come and go as they please—for the price of their merest attention. They're a parasite, and you're their host.

But, my love, you deserve better than that. Depending on our "desirability," our childhood experiences, friendships, relationships, and trauma, we've all received different messages about what kind of love we deserve. Please know that no matter what you've been told to believe about yourself, the toxic kind of love you may have been conditioned to "accept," or whatever it is that society has brainwashed you into believing, you are no one's fucking doormat. Start turning away people who have the audacity to show up in your life with crumbs, because crumbs can't feed you. Find someone who brings you a whole cake or, better yet, learn to make the cake yourself.

Learning how to love yourself, to avoid relying on other people's validation to make you feel whole, is the key to not settling. Because when you already have a delicious fucking cake, the idea of someone else's crumbs and settling for a mediocre love that leaves you starving ceases to be tempting. Refuse to settle for less than you deserve! Ensure that you have everything you could possibly need, supplied to and from yourself.

The process of being single and dating to me is very much like making my own cake. Refining the recipe, learning which ingredients I like the taste of, and which ruin the mix, so that I will always have enough to fill and satisfy my desires without the aid of someone else.

You are the love of your own life. Make your own cake.

CHAPTER 4

HOW TO BREAK UP WITH YOURSELF

Growth involves breaking up with yourself. (That's what makes it so bloody uncomfortable.)

We have become all too attached to our suffering strategies, to the narratives we keep telling ourselves, and to repeating self-sabotaging behavior. We find it easier to blame others and the world around us than to question how much of our pain is caused by subconsciously choosing this suffering because it's a lovely, familiar state of being.

An example of a comfortable, self-sabotaging narrative that I have indulged in myself: "I'm such an empath that my positive energy attracts people into my life who just want to use me." People used me when the narrative I believed was that bad people "wandered" into my life because I'm a healing, empathic, positive person. This was comfortable for me, because it meant I didn't have to change. But sticking to this way of thinking just prolongs suffering. What I actually needed to do was to learn how to set and hold boundaries.

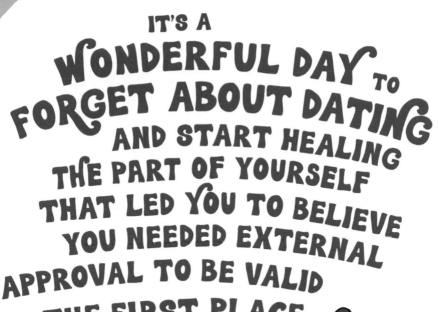

IT'S A **WONDERFUL DAY** TO **FORGET ABOUT DATING** AND START HEALING THE PART OF YOURSELF THAT LED YOU TO BELIEVE YOU NEEDED EXTERNAL APPROVAL TO BE VALID IN THE FIRST PLACE.

SOMETIMES THE PERSON STOPPING YOU FROM REACHING YOUR POTENTIAL ALL ALONG WAS YOUR OWN SUBCONSCIOUS ADDICTED TO THE COMFORT THAT COMES FROM BLAMING OTHERS.

IT'S TIME TO GET OUT OF YOUR OWN WAY.

As humans, we don't really want to find out whether any of our suffering has to do with us. After all, who would choose suffering? But growth requires accountability, and accountability is questioning whether "bad people" might actually be wandering into your life because they're attracted to your lack of boundaries and staying in your life because you're afraid of conflict. The kind of love you accept into your life is a reflection of the love that deep down you think you deserve. Low self-esteem doesn't mean you deserve bad treatment, and accountability is not about victim blaming (see page 56). Accountability means acknowledging to yourself what parts of you need healing. Questioning and interrogating yourself is paramount to escaping these destructive patterns and cycles of behavior.

In order to grow, you have to thank your old self, trust you deserve better, say goodbye, and move on.

You have to be willing to accept that sometimes you are self-sabotaging. Pointing the finger at those around you isn't going to bring about real and lasting change. You have to be held accountable for growth; you have to be willing to alter your perception and break up with the version of yourself that you have been clinging to for so long. You have to say goodbye to that former self-protective shell and accept that it's played its role in your life, but you have now outgrown it. You need to build a better, bigger version for you to evolve into the person you are becoming.

CHAPTER 5

REFUSE TO FIND COMFORT IN OTHER WOMEN'S FLAWS

Internalized misogyny is the silent, insidious killer of progress, and when it shows up in our lives it can make us act out in all kinds of ugly ways.

First things first, "flaws" aren't really there.
Flaws are manmade. And yes, I mean *man*made.

They're seeds planted in our minds by manipulative power systems, to make us feel so insecure that we buy products that promise we will become more acceptable, more desirable. The beauty standards of our society are racist, fatphobic, ageist, and, quite frankly, confusing. The things you feel most insecure about in your body are more than likely a direct result of capitalism because it works very hard to make sure that you will never feel enough without spending money. The models we see promoting these products and advertising this image of perceived flawlessness don't even look like that themselves. Their skin has been airbrushed, their bodies manipulated, and their features enhanced. In a lot of cases, Black women's skin is lightened and their features dramatically altered in post-production to make them look more European and perpetuate the colonialist ideas that equate whiteness with beauty.

As a result of the rigorous beauty standards that we are so harshly held up against, we inevitably find a disturbing amount of comfort in tearing down women who reflect our own insecurities back to us. The drive to become "more beautiful" for male consumption (and capitalist profit) creates a toxic competitiveness among women. How can we happily exist in a world that is built on systems that seek to tear us down?

The internalized misogynist will tell you that women shouldn't do certain things. I used to hate the shit out of hot, confident bisexual women. Why? Because I was jealous that they got to live their truth! It was so threatening and frightening to my heteronormative understanding of myself. Seeing them thrive and dating whoever they wanted; how dare they! They were everything I wanted to be but couldn't be, because I had placed limitations on myself. I projected the shame around my sexuality onto the women who were confident enough to own theirs. I hated that these women were living the life I wanted, but I didn't realize that was the reason until I had finally accepted and embraced my own sexuality.

Once you heal your insecurities, get to the root of where they originate, and identify the parts of yourself that you're ashamed of, you reframe your perspective and open the door to a wonderful thing called empathy.

It is through years of retraining that I have minimized the power internalized misogyny has over my thoughts. We seek comfort in other women's perceived "flaws" in an attempt to avoid addressing our own insecurities. The toxic ideas that have been planted in our minds keep us competing with each other, preventing us from growing and discovering our innate divine power.

Every time you catch yourself critiquing a woman on the choices she makes—who she sleeps with, how she dresses—sit in it. Reflect. What is it about her that makes you feel so uncomfortable? Perhaps she actually just reminds you of yourself, or the parts of yourself that you are ashamed of. Or perhaps she's the very person you want to be. Or perhaps you're like me and you actually just really fancy her and need to go ask her out.

Ask yourself why you think this way, instead of just accepting it. Reprogram your patriarchal brainwashing. The girl you're jealous and hateful of isn't a "bitch"—your internalized misogynist is.

EXAMPLES OF INTERNALIZED MISOGYNY

Here are some key examples of what internalized misogyny looks like, and how to handle it when it pops up in your brain:

You find yourself saying "I'm not like the other girls."
Think about what you are implying the other girls "are like" when you say this. If you are reinforcing stereotypes that women are "bitchy" or "full of drama" and that you are the exception, darling, you are not. Stereotypes sit at the bottom of a pyramid, and they fuel the bigger problems at the top, like gendered violence towards women (it sounds dramatic, but it isn't). Don't perpetuate the cycle.

CHEERS!

TO TAKING OWNERSHIP OF OUR HEALING,
AND NO LONGER JUDGING OTHERS
IN AN ATTEMPT TO FEEL
IN CONTROL OF OUR
OWN INSECURITIES.

You constantly find ways to tear down successful women.
We truly despise people who remind us of the parts of our lives we wish we were thriving in but aren't. Be careful not to fall into the habit of tearing down other women to make yourself feel better. The satisfaction will wear off and you'll be back to facing those unaddressed insecurities. Leave her alone; let her shine!

No, you don't have to like all women—don't put that pressure on yourself. You do not have to uplift, empower, or make friends with someone who you don't get along with just because they are a woman. The key is to learn to recognize whether the problem is actually her or whether it's your own insecurities. Take note of the things that make you want to tear her down. Are you jealous that she's running a thriving business? Go home, write a list of all the things that bring you joy, and figure out how they can make you a profit. Are you pissed that she has lots of cool, like-minded friends? My love, get on the internet! Follow pages with your interests and try to build an online community of like-minded people who you could potentially meet IRL. Is she always putting together incredible looks; is her makeup on point? Start watching those YouTube tutorials! Does the fact that she has a similar style irritate you? Great minds think alike; why not pitch a collaboration instead?

If we can learn to view other women as opportunities for inspiration and empowerment in our own lives and realize that there is enough room for all of us to be happy, the relationships and bonds we form together will be unstoppable.

You hate your partner's ex.
Being in a relationship with someone who has an ex-girlfriend is the perfect opportunity to wrestle through our internalized misogyny. This is possibly the most heightened that our internalized hatred of other women can ever become. Why? Because we literally put ourselves in an imaginary competition with our partner's ex. And with social media, you can end up comparing yourself with every single aspect of her online life or, worse yet, actively trying to seek out flaws for temporary relief to make yourself feel better. It's awful, and it's ugly.

But don't worry; you've got this. It's a great opportunity for you to work on strengthening the love you have for yourself and, as a result, other women!

You say, "She's a slut."
But is she actually just exercising her right to bodily autonomy? Regardless, it's none of your business.

Ask yourself if you would say the same thing about a man. These pernicious stereotypes are largely saved for women, and when we badmouth other women for expressing their sexuality, we feed into the narrative that women have no agency over their own bodies. Whatever women choose to do with their sex lives, it's never your business. In a society that turns women into objects, who are you to judge people who find empowerment in the very narrative that tries to demean their humanity?

You say, "She's so bossy and intimidating!"
When a woman asserts her boundaries and says "no" to things, she's not being bossy. She is doing exactly what she has to do to protect her energy and GET. SHIT. DONE. Ask yourself this question: "Is she intimidating, or am I intimidated?" (see page 52).

Is she bossy or is she just acting outside of the submissive stereotype that society has convinced you she needs to be? Women are socialized to constantly pander to the needs of everyone else but themselves, and even if we do decide to take care of ourselves, we are encouraged to do it in the form of "retail therapy" or "beauty rituals" that still pander to our appearance instead of our mental health.

Respect women who set firm boundaries; don't see doing so as a threat. She's worked really fucking hard to get to a point in her life where she has decided to choose her happiness over people-pleasing. Remind yourself that there is no one way to be a woman, and tell your internalized misogynist to shut the hell up!

Maybe she's a "bitch," or maybe her ability to unapologetically set boundaries makes you uncomfortable because it forces you to acknowledge that you are a doormat in your own life.

. . . Maybe.

You judge other women on their appearance.
When my own judgmental thoughts make an appearance, I flip them around and say the opposite. Empower others instead of judging them—practicing empathy can change the world.

For example:

- You see a woman walking down the street in a miniskirt and your immediate thought is that she should be dressing "more carefully." Flip it around: instead, say, "Her clothes aren't the problem—the problem is rapists and their predatory behavior towards women's bodies."
- You see an older woman rocking a tight dress she ordered off Urban Outfitters in the club and your first thought is, "Bloody hell! She's too old for that!" Flip it around: instead, say, "Wow, in spite of ageism and the sexist idea that women past

a certain age shouldn't love and flaunt their bodies, this woman decided to just go for it anyway! What a fucking legend."

- You see a woman who covers herself up (for religious or nonreligious purposes, neither of which are your business) and your immediate assumption is that she must be "prudish" and "unempowered." Flip it around: instead, say, "Different things empower different people— there is no one way to be a woman. Women are multifaceted human beings capable of being more than one thing at the same time."

- You comment on butch women/masc women's appearance because of their lack of femininity. Flip it around: instead, say, "Wow, in spite of the expectation for women to constantly cater to the male gaze, these butch ICONS are choosing to express their gender in a way that feels most authentic to themselves."

- You judge or pity divorced women. Flip it around: instead, say, "Divorced women successfully escaped a situation in which they were unhappy. I hope I have the courage to do the same if I ever find myself in a similar situation."

- You make comments on Black women's hair or use words such as "bossy" or "aggressive" to describe Black women in power. Flip it around: instead, say, "I have been conditioned by a white supremacist society to unconsciously hold racist views about how women of color should appear and behave. Any unsolicited comments on how Black women choose to live their lives or carry themselves are both misogynistic and racist. Full stop."

I could go on forever. But when it comes to judging other people, ask yourself if what they are doing is affecting you. If it isn't, we must learn to move the fuck on with our lives.

You judge other women who pay for cosmetic procedures.
Would it be incredible if we lived in a world where women didn't feel the need to adhere to sexist beauty standards and go under the knife to get closer to those standards? You're goddamn right it would. But that world doesn't yet exist. Which is why we must fight to make it exist instead of blaming women for trying to thrive within the framework that is currently on offer.

You find yourself saying things like "She looks good for her age."
Ageism is a heavily gendered issue. It seems that any woman past the age of twenty-five has an urgency placed on her by society to rush and find a husband before she's "old, wrinkly, and infertile."

When was the last time you heard of a man exclaiming that he must find a bride before he gets old and gray? There is a societal time limit placed on women, as our value as human beings is tied to our physical "beauty." The older we get, the less valuable we are to society. The next time you find yourself commenting on a woman in relation to her appearance, abilities, or, God forbid, her fertility, stop. Ask yourself if you would say the same thing about a man.

MAYBE IT'S TENSION; MAYBE YOU'RE PROJECTING

It's a big thing to be able to admit your own shortcomings and actively work to stop your own insecurities from affecting other people. Try as often as possible to operate from a nonjudgmental place and catch yourself when you project your issues on others. We all do it; we're all human.

Your character is not to be judged by the mistakes you make—but by your ability to hold yourself accountable, interrogate your actions, and come back with the correct behavior.

THERE IS **ENOUGH ROOM** FOR ALL **WOMEN** TO BE WHOLE WITHOUT TEARING EACH OTHER DOWN.

CHAPTER 6

ARE THEY INTIMIDATING, OR AM I INTIMIDATED?

The way people treat you is absolutely no reflection on you or your value.

A lot of how we treat one another is based on assumptions. These assumptions may be informed by a whole host of cultural biases—racism, transphobia, homophobia, etc.—and also our own insecurities. This is not to excuse people's shitty behavior, but if you can master the art of not internalizing other people's insecurities (aka not giving a shit what people think or say about you), you will live a much more peaceful, authentic life.

The perfect example of projection is how people can interpret the same piece of artwork in many different ways, based on their different lived experiences and tastes. Because art is subjective. Art is usually a reflection of our inner truth, and sharing this work can make us feel quite exposed. It feels like an extension of an artist's self. I used to take criticism so personally for this reason, because my artwork is quite literally an amalgamation of my experiences and personal style, churned out for the world to see in the form of illustrations and essays so other people can learn from my mistakes. Sharing my art can make me feel very vulnerable.

But my perspective changed completely when I realized that no matter what anyone says about my art, the art remains the same. It doesn't actually change! It blew my damn mind. Your perception of it may have changed, but the art itself has stayed the same the whole time.

> **When people say cruel things, consider what is said but also who is saying it and where that criticism might originate, what it might be rooted in.**

If I hadn't really internalized the truth that people bring their own insecurities and prejudices to their critiques about others and had instead taken their criticism as objective feedback, I wouldn't be making art for myself anymore. I'd be a people-pleasing puppet, allowing other people's tastes and motivations to dictate the work I was creating.

When I first started putting out my politically charged artwork on the internet at the age of seventeen, it felt like I was carving out a piece of my mind and laying it bare for everyone to see. But more and more women gradually came forward telling me that they related to the experiences I was discussing, and before I knew it, I had created a small community of people wanting to feel empowered, shedding the shame they had been carrying around for simply existing in this world. If I didn't choose to leave

MAYBE I'M "TOO MUCH"; MAYBE MY ABUNDANCE JUST REMINDS YOU THAT YOU'RE LACKING.

my comfort zone and be loud about the things I care about, I wouldn't be writing this book and I wouldn't have embarked on the greatest journey of my life.

If someone tells you that you're "too much," it's because they don't feel enough. If someone tells you that you're "too sensitive," it's because deep down they envy your ability to be vulnerable, your capacity to feel, and the freedom you give yourself to express your feelings. Hurt people hurt people.

Stop breaking yourself down into bite-sized pieces. Stay whole and let them choke.

PEOPLE-PLEASING—STOP WANTING TO BE LIKED

Choosing yourself will always disappoint some people. The sooner we accept this and make peace with it, the better.

People who do not have a strong sense of self will constantly change to reflect their surroundings and the people they are with. People pleasers change who they are constantly, and each time they do, they silence an authentic part of themselves to be something else, for someone else. How sad is that? Over time, the body gets used to ignoring its own instincts and desires, resulting in cripplingly low self-esteem as we repeatedly put others first and tell ourselves that our own needs don't matter. We are all multifaceted human beings who "code-switch" sometimes. For a lot of marginalized people, code-switching and learning to assimilate to the dominant culture (white, straight, cis) is necessary to be met with basic human respect, but everyone sometimes chooses to show different sides of ourselves to our parents, coworkers, friends, and romantic partners. However, compromising or adapting parts of your identity, beliefs, and personality to be liked by someone is neither healthy nor sustainable, and, quite frankly, it's exhausting. Performing femininity is exhausting enough, so why give yourself the added pressure of another layer of performance? You cannot win, and the world will judge you either way. Feel empowered and not defeated by this truth—it means that the only available option is to be yourself.

Compromising to form relationships and friendships doesn't work because they will be based on a false connection anyway. Present exactly what you want and need, and if they can't match it, then at least you know.

DON'T PROJECT BACK WHAT HAS BEEN PROJECTED ONTO YOU

Painful things happen. But if we leave past experiences unchecked, we can end up unintentionally inflicting the same pain onto other people as a coping mechanism. We are all responsible for our own healing, and it's in your power how you choose to let it impact your life and the lives of those around you. You have to be responsible for the way you treat others, despite what has happened to you. It is your responsibility not to project your trauma, past experiences, and insecurities onto other people.

**This is not victim blaming;
this is accountability.**

Sometimes projection manifests itself physically. People build entire lives, spin false narratives, and accumulate material possessions to fill the void caused by their insecurities or guilt. What they really need is therapy. We all have insecurities, but it is our responsibility not to inflict them on others and cause further suffering.

The next time you think about commenting on someone else's appearance, catch yourself and consider why you feel the need to do

WHEN YOU HAVE **LIVED A LIFE** OF PEOPLE-PLEASING, OWNING YOUR TRUE DESIRES **WILL MAKE YOU FEEL GUILTY.** PUSH THROUGH AND COMMUNICATE THEM. YOU DIDN'T COME HERE TO BE LIKED.

this. Keep your unwarranted commentaries about other people's lives to yourself, work through why you feel the need to gossip about others in the first place, heal those wounds, and come back with correct behavior.

I hate engaging in spiteful gossip, so if one of my friends starts to tell me something I don't want to hear about, I try to say, "That's not our business; let's not be those people." It holds a mirror to that person and gently asks them to reflect. Not everyone takes this easily, especially as gossip is one of the things women are encouraged to "bond" over. You'll often be met with a defensive reaction from friends, but this person has been faced with their truth (that gossiping is ugly and a reflection of their inner reality). You want to get to a point in your life where gossiping is genuinely unenjoyable. I no longer enjoy forming bonds with people at the expense of exchanging information about other people's lives. It isn't healthy, and it says more about how those gossiping view themselves than the qualities of the person in discussion. Surround yourself with people who have an open mind, people who are open to learning from you, and people whose perspectives you are open to listening to also. We all mess up every now and then, but you must remember to do the work.

Think back to a time when you said something you didn't believe in, for the temporary satisfaction that another person would feel connected to you. Analyze why you did this, and, babe—*don't do that shit again.*

For example, one of the times that I shrunk myself down for approval was at the beginning of my feminist journey, by "dampening down" my feminism around men. I would water down my ideas and feel disgusted at myself, as I found that their reaction to my watered-down feminism was feeding my internalized

misogynist, making myself out to
be "not like those other feminists" for
their temporary approval.

When it's safe to, being your authentic self
forces people to reveal whether they deserve a place
in your life or not. This truth is a gift and will save you a lot
of energy. Stop breaking down. Stay whole.

CHAPTER 7

STOP SCROLLING IN THE MORNINGS

If it weren't for social media:
- I wouldn't know some of my closest friends
- I would not be "out" as a queer woman (at least not at this stage in my life)
- I would not have had the chance to meet and date lots of queer people
- I would not have found the tools to spot abusive behaviors in relationships
- I would not have gotten myself into therapy
- I would not have been given the opportunity to write the book you are reading

These are just a few powerful ways social media has positively impacted my life, and how I have harnessed its vast catalogue of information and perspectives to liberate myself from toxic situations and embark on my journey of growth and understanding myself.

As someone whose IRL community was nonexistent, I was aching for conversations that challenged me and my perception of reality. To put it simply, I despised stagnancy, and I craved growth. I still do. I got a taste of that when I started to vocalize my experiences and my opinions online. I couldn't believe there were other teenagers out there as fed up with the same bullshit as I was. And I couldn't believe the sheer number of voices I'd never heard from before or come across in the world I inhabited—people whose perspectives would become invaluable to my understanding of not just the systems of oppression that I was suffering under but ones that I benefitted from too. Influencers, educators, therapists, and artists have taught me more valuable lessons online about the world and myself than I was ever afforded during my formal education in school.

Social media amplified the voices of marginalized people who weren't usually represented (or represented fairly) in the mainstream media that I consumed. This was a space where people got to represent themselves on their own terms. For the first time, I could seek out bisexual, queer femmes living their best lives, people of color talking openly about their experiences with racism, art from those across the broad spectrum of sexuality and gender. It helped me unpack my fatphobia, thanks to the people who highlighted the bias inherent in the way I only illustrated thin bodies. I learned the importance of accountability through trained therapists online, and here I am today, still learning. I have utilized Instagram as a mirror, and the work of its creators has given me an in-depth reflection to better and more thoroughly understand myself. It's a space I have used to influence others and allowed others to influence me. If we want social media to positively impact our lives and use it as a catalyst for growth, we must make a conscious effort to diversify and declutter our feeds.

REPROGRAM YOUR PATRIARCHAL BRAINWASHING

Your preferences are political. The way you view yourself and others is informed by the narratives and stereotypes you consume about the world through the media.

Social media gives us a chance to deprogram our preference for disgustingly racist, patriarchal, and Western standards of beauty. A fantastic example of a movement dedicated to revising our idea of beauty is Chidera Eggerue's hashtag #SaggyBoobsMatter, which has empowered people to cancel their surgery appointments for breast reduction/lifting. Another is #TransIsBeautiful, which highlights the spectrum of trans identities and positions them in an empowering light, as opposed to dehumanization and sexualization. There are multitudes of pages dedicated to uplifting fat bodies, fashion blogs for physically disabled people, and queer couples just living their best lives. When mainstream media is overwhelmingly straight, cisgender, able-bodied, and white, consuming this content is oxygen to me.

Search for empowering, educational, therapeutic Instagram accounts, and look for ones run by Black people, trans people, and queer people—there are so many articles and websites that highlight the best ones. Doesn't it sound nice to get lost in a social media hole that feels empowering and challenging, and that encourages inner growth rather than sending you into a spiral of self-deprecation and comparison? These people will probably teach you as much about yourself as your formal schooling—so remember to pay people for the education they give you when you can. Most people have links to their PayPal or Patreon on their pages!

**Your happiness—the way you view yourself—
and the content you consume is in your control.
Make changes. Now.**

IT'S
NOT FAIR
ON YOUR MIND TO COMPARE
YOUR LOWEST MOMENTS
TO ANOTHER PERSON'S
HIGHLIGHT REEL,
ESPECIALLY
FIRST THING
IN THE
MORNING.

INSTANT GRATIFICATION IS A BOTTOMLESS PIT

However much I have gained and benefited from utilizing Instagram as a platform, if left unchecked and un-moderated, its use can be detrimental to my mental health and self-image. If the foundation of our happiness and how we think about ourselves relies on the validation we receive from strangers on the internet, it is not real, lasting, and fulfilling happiness. But we already knew that, because every time we upload content that doesn't get the usual amount of comments and likes, we're left feeling like a pile of unvalidated shit. Don't be fooled; this is all a very intentional effect of social media.

Sean Parker (the cofounder of Facebook) admitted that addiction is, in fact, not just a by-product of social media—it's part of the design. Just like gambling, the unpredictability of social media is what makes it so addictive. Not knowing the outcome of a post becomes a high, and each time we receive a positive response, our body releases endorphins to make us feel an overwhelming (but fleeting) sense of validation and excitement. The more frequently we engage with this algorithm, the more we learn to crave the next adrenaline rush.

Most of us are shackled to our devices. I know that my attention span and ability to focus on a task have reduced dramatically since I began using social media. I check my phone like clockwork even when it hasn't made a noise, I check my socials first thing in the morning and before I go to bed, I obsess over who has and hasn't liked my pictures and what that means, and I've projected my insecurities onto the comments that people have left on my posts, sending my mind into anxiety overdrive.

We all have a void that we're trying to fill, and social media assists in widening that void. Social media and the internet create a dependency.

It took me awhile to notice the pattern, but when we are triggered by something, or when we feel low, we try to fill that void—quickly. What our void really needs is tending to; it needs love, and it needs to heal. That void needs therapy.

But with instant gratification increasingly accessible, we find ourselves regularly settling for the quick fix. We are living at peak content consumption, with a demand for instant services. Literally anything you want. You need an outfit for tomorrow night? You can have it delivered to your door the same day. Craving a shag? There's an app for that. Need your makeup done for a last-minute event? Again, there's an app for that! You can order a masseuse, hair stylist, or four-star meal to your door, within the hour.

It can be hard at times to allow ourselves to be slow in this world. Social media and the internet aren't going to disappear completely, and we wouldn't want them to. But just like everything we engage with, we need to set and hold firm boundaries to be able to get what we want out of it. Here are a few limits that have worked for me and allowed me to get the best out of social media and reduce some of the harmful effects it can have on my mental health:

- Turn your phone off sometimes! Or, if you can't turn it off, temporarily delete your social apps.
- Turn notifications on silent so you're not tempted to keep frantically checking your phone like clockwork.
- Put your phone in your kitchen/living room before you go to bed to stop the urge to scroll late at night and when you wake up. It's not fair on your mind to compare your lowest moments with another person's highlight reel, especially first thing in the morning.
- You are allowed to unfollow people. If they make you feel like shit about yourself, unfollow them. Or mute them. Work through why those feelings come up for you and why this person

makes you feel uncomfortable. Maybe it's nothing to do with them; maybe it's you. Different people evoke different emotions in us—acknowledge these feelings and use them as a catalyst for growth and self-knowledge.

- Follow accounts that encourage your growth and make you want to align with your highest self. Accounts that trash other women, promote an unhealthy dieting culture, or are triggering for your mental health are going to keep you stagnant, suffering, and stuck in old patterns.

- Unapologetically block trolls and people who are harassing you. People on the internet do not get to dictate your happiness with spiteful projections of their insecurities. So often we can obsess over another person's comments and internalize something that's actually just a projection of their own insecurity. It's not about you. Don't take on someone else's problem.

- If you have a community on Instagram, set boundaries on your engagement with it. Take time to think about what you have energy for and tell your community what you will and won't be doing. This will also help you decide who to block, as people who don't respect your boundaries don't deserve access to your space. In my own social media communities, I don't give people advice when they ask for it in my DMs because (1) I'm not trained, (2) I'm not being paid to do that, and (3) I don't work for free. I'm not a source of empowerment for people who have no intention of reciprocating that energy. Emotional labor is still labor.

PRESSURE TO PERFORM

If who you are changes and shifts depending on "what works well for the algorithm," how long is it going to be before that version of yourself is what you feel unable to "live up to" in real life? We all compare ourselves with capitalist beauty standards, but it seems that with our highly curated lives on Instagram, we have created yet another impossible standard—the curated version of our life that we present online.

We put up the best bits of our lives on Instagram: the days our hair and makeup are looking good, when we're on vacation, when we're out with our friends, when we have had professional successes. It's all a very surface-level presentation of what our lives actually look like because we are projecting only the good moments to the world. A few things people don't see about my life are the therapy appointments from which I run home crying, the mornings I struggle to get out of bed, the trash that still needs taking out, and the fact I haven't cooked myself a proper meal for over a month. But what do we actually "owe" our audience? Do we owe them anything?

You don't owe anyone your trauma. Social media can sometimes make it feel like we owe it to people to share with them the most intimate details of our lives in the name of "transparency"—but why cut yourself open and show the most vulnerable, unhealed, and intimate parts of yourself if it feels uncomfortable? Opening up and being vulnerable should be reserved for times when it will benefit your healing—not for the sake of other people feeling entitled to know about your business. The view people have into my life is already incredibly intimate. People have seen the inside of my apartment; they know who my friends are, what clothes I wear day to day; they know what makes me laugh . . . but people are not entitled to anything beyond what I choose to share.

There is a compulsion to record, capture, and showcase our moments of joy with the world on social media. But you deserve to keep some things for yourself.

"I AM NOT RESPONSIBLE FOR THE IDEA THAT YOU HAVE CREATED OF ME IN YOUR MIND"

If we're not careful, we can find ourselves using people on Instagram as screens for our projections and insecurities. Although we only see about 5 percent of their curated lives, still we project our own insecurities, shortcomings, fears, unhealed trauma, and romanticized ideas about people to fill the gaps in what we know about them. Then, would you believe, we feel entitled to be disappointed when they don't turn out to be this person we made them out to be! I hate to break it to you, but people on Instagram don't owe you a thing. There's a certain amount of entitlement that we all have when it comes to the people we interact with and follow online. We want to know who they're dating, who they're friends with, where they like to go to eat, what places they frequent. We can begin to see them not as flesh-and-blood people but as free, consumable content.

Name one person who is both happy and successful who got to where they are by obsessing over other people's fabricated lives on Instagram . . .

I'll wait.

CHAPTER 8

PROTECT YOUR ENERGY

Your time and energy should be preserved, above all, for yourself. Anyone who wants to be a part of your life must be an addition to your wholeness. If you are subconsciously seeking someone to "make you whole," you're not ready for a relationship.

Sure, relationships can add to our happiness by being sources of love and support. But if you put your worth and happiness exclusively into another person, the moment you part ways you'll be left with the same unhealed wounds you started off with, now with an additional person-shaped void to fill too.

When we use other people to make us feel whole, we start to equate our value with how they treat us, and we can end up losing our sense of inherent self-worth. We cannot take it as a personal fault or a reflection of our worthiness when others project their own internalized suffering onto us by mistreating us or leaving us. Prioritize the love you have for yourself so much that if a relationship ends, you aren't left feeling diminished. Because you already have a firm sense of who you are, and you know that you are more than enough on your own.

Think about the person you could become if you stopped searching for value in your ability to fix others, and put that energy into yourself and your own life. Imagine the sheer power and confidence you would radiate! Imagine.

When you choose to focus on yourself, the things you once craved and the people from whom you once desperately needed validation will cease to become necessary. You will realize you no longer need them. In fact, you never did. They were all temporary distractions from the real love of your life: yourself.

You don't have time in this life to be wasting precious energy on people who don't even realize what a privilege it is to be in your life. If they can't see how bloody fantastic you are, why would you want to be with them anyway? Those people simply do not deserve to know you.

Move on.

To practice self-love and protect your energy, you need to start implementing boundaries with the people you surround yourself with. Remember: those who do not respect your boundaries do not deserve to know you.

Simple boundaries to start with include:
- Saying "no."
- Speaking up when someone is making you feel uncomfortable.
- If you need alone time, say so. You don't have to justify it.
- Delegating tasks and saying "yes" to help from others.

Questions to ask yourself daily as a way of checking in:
- Am I going to this event because I want to, or because I feel external pressure to?
- Do I have the capacity to help others right now?

- Do I follow the advice I give to others?
- If I could give myself one thing this week, what would it be?
- What am I putting off right now?
- Do I feel comfortable in this moment?
- How do the people currently in my life make me feel?
- Have I been allowing myself to feel my feelings lately, or have I been minimizing them?
- Have I expressed to people how I'm feeling?
- Are people respecting my identity/identities?

SETTING BOUNDARIES

I constantly implement new boundaries as I learn more about my desires and what makes me uncomfortable. People's responses to my boundary-setting reveals to me their emotional maturity. I had to be honest with myself and admit that part of me still believed my worth was tied up in pleasing others but that I must continuously work towards keeping myself and my needs at the fore. When I began setting boundaries and checking in with myself, I became aware of how I felt after spending time with certain people; it forced me to think about myself first and protect my energy.

My friends and I are obsessed with respecting each other and learning about one another's boundaries—and I don't think there's a love more important and beautiful than that.

WHAT BOUNDARIES DO YOU NEED TO PUT IN PLACE TO PROTECT YOUR OWN ENERGY?

Here are a few boundaries that will help you assess whether the people in your life respect you and deserve you:

Do you feel that you're able to say "no" to them?

"No" is the most definable, clear, and communicative boundary, yet we often find ourselves feeling guilty for saying "no" to people, even when it comes at the expense of our own comfort and desires. Agreeing to favors for friends when you want to and pushing yourself out of your comfort zone to experience something new and exciting is entirely different. That's what friends are for—growth! But it's a red flag when you feel like you might experience some form of guilt or punishment from someone for simply telling them "no." Using the fact you said "no" to get you to do things for them in the future, becoming passive-aggressive with silent treatment, cutting off communication, and ignoring your messages to make you feel guilty, for example, are all forms of emotional manipulation. Work on healing the parts of yourself that thought you deserved this kind of treatment. Inspect those wounds.

How does this person make you feel after seeing them?

If you're left feeling drained and depleted of energy, if their company brings out a bad side of you, or if you feel like you're agreeing to things you don't want to, then they're waving a big old red flag right in your face. They're practically smacking you in the face with it, hun. Refuse to give the limited amount of time you have in this life to people who bring out the worst version of you.

Does this person value your time?

Time is another important boundary and a real eye-opener. If someone always shows up late, cancels last minute, and only drops in your life when they need you, they do not respect your time. This is not a reciprocal relationship. You are being used for your energy! Don't give any time to people who don't have time for you.

GASLIGHTING

Gaslighting—when someone's lived experiences are deflected and they're made to doubt their own perception—is a form of emotional manipulation that often plays out in abusive relationships and can cause victims to lose their sense of self almost entirely. Gaslighting often leaves its victims questioning their own reality. Here are some examples:

Straight-up lying

Say you saw the person you're dating kiss someone else in a bar, you confront them about it the next morning, and they tell you they were in all evening watching TV and that you must be "going mad." Or they say something hurtful to you and, when you bring it up at a later date, they deny ever saying it without leaving the slightest room for possibility that they might have just forgotten. "Nope, I never said that. That's in your head. Why would I say that to you?" If it gets to the point where you feel like you actually need to record interactions with someone, run. Really. If they have you doubting yourself this much, you're more than likely dealing with a narcissist. Get the hell outta there!

Denial of your lived experiences

Let's say a Black man is recalling a time he was stopped and searched on his way into a nightclub, but none of the white guys he was with were. He's confiding in his white friend about this experience, and his friend says, "Not everything's about race; don't play that card. It was probably a random check." This is a form of gaslighting: making him question if his own experience really was all in his head.

Calling you "crazy"

Their aim with this word is to manipulate you to the point of doubting your own reality so much that you accept their invented reality instead.

They may also call you "crazy" to other people so that if you were ever to seek help from others, they would have already built a case that you're too "psycho" or "crazy" to be trusted. They have a better chance of keeping you manipulated if they can isolate you.

BE SMART WITH YOUR ENERGY. TREAT IT LIKE THE CURRENCY OF YOUR BUSINESS.

Check in with yourself and others regularly to encourage the preservation of energy in your friendship groups. Help each other to prioritize and preserve your resources. Resources could be anything from time to energy to money. Whatever it is, whatever form it takes, big or small—put yourself first.

Your energy is a limited resource. If you're spending too much doing things for other people and spreading yourself too thin, let your friends know that you simply don't have the capacity to meet them this week. Make sure you always have enough energy in your bank, as if it were your savings. Keep an eye on what's coming in and what's going out: how much you give to others, and how much you receive yourself. You cannot run on empty, the same way a business cannot be profitable if it doesn't bring in more money than it spends.

Women are constantly expected to be "nice." What that really means is "perform emotional labor for free." If you don't conform? You're a bitch. When people call me a "bitch" or say that I'm "intimidating," all I hear is the sound of their own insecurities and lack of self-worth, because I used to be that person—the doormat being walked over by everyone in my life, resenting those who were able to set boundaries. Respect yourself and your energy more than freely giving it to people who have no intention of reciprocating. Don't devalue yourself like that.

Stop saying "sure" to everything when really you mean "no." If protecting your energy and refusing to entertain things that don't nourish your soul makes you a "bitch"—then go ahead, be a bitch.

CHAPTER 9

TO DATE OR NOT TO DATE

There is so much power in knowing what you do and don't want from life, and dating someone new is an opportunity for you to practice setting your boundaries and protecting your energy. Going on dates, whether they turn out well or not, offers endless possibilities to learn about all the different sides of yourself.

Before going on a first date with someone, you must remember that on first dates everyone will only be shining a light on the most attractive facets of themselves and presenting their best bits. There's a number of other sides of them you know nothing about, full of history, past relationships, behaviors, and trauma.

This is why looking out for red flags on the first date is crucial. View a first date like an interview—you're both trying to see if you could work well together. That's not to say you should barrage your date with intimidating questions, but it's important to keep in mind that you're not the only one who has to make a good impression. Would you interrupt someone in an interview to use your phone? Would you show up late? Would you hire someone who was late? If they're already exhibiting toxic patterns of behavior, oversharing, or checking their phone constantly—what are they going to be like when they're *comfortable*?

We accept the love we think we deserve. It's hard to do—but part of growing is acknowledging the uncomfortable truth that, although we do not deserve bad treatment, abuse in our society is normalized. When something is normalized, we accept it and it remains unchallenged. We settle for mediocre partners because we don't believe we deserve better. If left unchecked, we can end up subconsciously seeking partners who require the care and attention that really we wish we could give to ourselves. This is a form of projection that neglects the healing that we need to do ourselves by instead spending our time trying to fix others. Your willingness and urge to fix everyone and direct that energy away from yourself is a sign you have wounds to heal that you're ignoring. Go tend to them.

"When someone shows you who they are, believe them the first time."

They might be hot, but if they're a piece of shit, *they're a piece of shit*. Learn to let go of people at the first sight of a red flag, before you even contemplate compromising yourself and your standards. Demanding better for yourself is hard, especially because at times it will be lonely. But whenever you're tempted to settle, remember: you date someone's emotional maturity, not their jawline. Ignoring your red flags or "deal breakers" will be the reason things don't work out in the long run anyway.

We're not settling for crumbs, ever.

Remember?

I once went on a first date with a man who was in therapy, was good looking, and had a thriving career—in short, he seemed very promising. That was until he brought up his ex and said he "can't date girls who spend too much time on their looks anymore." He followed this up by saying he doesn't believe in the wage gap. *You can only imagine the look on my face.* I told him right there and then that I didn't think we'd be compatible due to our different views, thanked him for the drink, and ordered my ride home. No time wasted trying to fix him. No wishful thinking that I could help "grow this man" into an open-minded feminist—I'm not looking for a project. You cannot fall in love with someone's "potential," hun. You're just kidding yourself, falling for a version of them that doesn't exist, and filling in the gaps in their character with what you want and need from them. But you can't change people. He showed me who he was, and I chose to love myself enough to believe him the first time.

"Stop asking yourself if you're good enough for people. Are they even good enough for you?"

We can get so wrapped up in how we are perceived by others on a date that we don't pay nearly enough attention to whether or not we even like them, or whether their attention is just propping up our ego, making us feel wanted. Don't get the two mixed up. As Wanda says in *BoJack Horseman*, "When you look at someone through rose-tinted glasses, all the red flags just look like flags."

Stay vigilant.

QUEER FIRST DATES

Queer first dates don't have a script and there are fewer gender roles at play, but a lot of my queer dates are hilariously formulaic. They usually involve talking shit about capitalism, finding out you've dated the same person, telling your coming-out story, talking for hours as you slowly edge closer to each other because no one wants to make the first move . . . it's beautiful. I love the experience of being able to be my fully blossomed self and not feeling the need to fulfill a prescribed gender role. The only issue is that often I find myself sitting there the entire time wondering . . .

"Is this a date or are we just hanging out?"

I wish someone had warned me how ambiguous queer dating can be. Not only do you have to find out if they're single, but you need to find out if they're even queer (which usually involves relentlessly scrolling through their Instagram page to find some form of a rainbow flag). And then you have to find out if they're into you or if they just want to be your friend.

With the amount of ambiguous "maybe dates" I've been on with women, I can tell you that it isn't worth the mental or physical energy "waiting to find out." Don't do it to yourself; you both need and deserve clarity. You're going to need to sharpen up on your communication skills if you want to navigate the queer dating scene (and not be confused the whole time). *Especially* if you're a femme! The world assumes that you're

straight because of the way you express your gender, and straight girls who "wanna go for a drink" don't realize how confusing that sentiment is to someone who wants to go for a drink . . . *and maybe back to your place afterwards.* Spare yourself the energy and communicate your desires directly.

"Do you want to go for a drink?" isn't always clear enough when it comes to dating other queer people of your same gender, especially if they have no clue you're also queer. If you're unsure, you're going to need to pointedly ask them if they'd like to go on a date with you. Or if they ask you—you're going to clarify with *them* if it's a date. The worst thing that could happen is that they say they're not queer, available, or interested! Asking people up front has strengthened my confidence and my ability to handle rejection. I'd much rather find out that someone is straight or simply not interested from the beginning and have a chat with my ego about that hit of rejection on my own time than go on a "maybe date," spending the whole time analyzing their body language, waiting for them to make a move, and going home even *more* confused than I was before. Being honest about what you want, and communicating it, is sexy as hell. It also makes life a lot more straightforward.

Protect your energy. *Ask them if it's a date.*

**"I no longer date when I'm vibrating at a low frequency.
It's like placing myself on a clearance rack."
—Necole Kane**

Crumbs are only tempting when you're hungry, so you must ensure that you're always full on your own. Avoid seeking out dates when you're feeling low or processing recent breakups—that's when you enter "settling for less than you deserve" territory, repeat cycles of self-destructive behavior, and end up dating people who simply don't deserve to know you. In the past, I've dated and entertained people who weren't good enough for me purely because I wasn't feeling good about myself. When we're not in a particularly stable place and we're feeling low, or we're at a place in our life when we're craving external validation, it can be very easy to get swept up in someone's allure and ignore red flags or controlling behaviors. This is when toxic relationships flourish.

You are in a far better position to date when you love yourself, because:

- You start to see your worth outside of being coupled with someone else's shared identity.
- You start to realize your worth as a unique and individual whole person, as opposed to someone else's "other half."
- You'll abstain from your need to settle, because you don't need someone to complete you. You complete you.
- You're more in touch with your needs and desires, so saying "no" to people who don't match your standards won't feel hard. It will feel like self-care. It will feel invigorating.

Add value to my life or bust.

I'm extra as hell with how I spend my energy, and I don't care what anyone thinks of that. I've had to get on my hands and knees to scrape my life back together far too many times to just allow any person to wander into my space again. When it comes to my life, there's no way I'm living it unchecked and without making sure I'm doing what's best for me. My boundaries are nonnegotiable.

After I once had a debilitating dating experience, I wrote up something I call "The Checklist" to ensure that I never compromise my standards and boundaries when it comes to someone new entering my life ever again. My checklist keeps me accountable.

These are a few things on my checklist:
- Does this person challenge me in a healthy way?
- Have they demonstrated that they respect my time?
- Are they a feminist?

I also have a list of red flags, including:
- Do they say things to me that I'd feel uncomfortable repeating to a friend?
- Do they only talk about themselves?
- Do they talk negatively of others for no reason?

. . . you get the picture.

So go write your version of "The Checklist." Of course, your list may look a lot different than mine. Do not try to apply my standards if they don't work for you. This is just my personal way to check in with myself, ensuring that I'm always receiving the treatment I want and deserve. Regardless of where I'm at with my self-esteem, I always deserve the best.

OUR DATING "PREFERENCES" ARE POLITICAL
"I don't date feminine guys."
"I have a thing for Asian girls."
"I don't like girls who are high-maintenance."
"I like girls who can be one of the guys."

BEING
HONEST
ABOUT WHAT
YOU WANT AND
COMMUNICATING IT
IS SEXY
AS HELL.

"I can't stand drama."

"I've only dated Black guys."

We all have preferences when it comes to dating people, whether for their looks, interests, career prospects, etc. But when it comes to someone's identity, our preferences when dating are inherently political. Most people assume we all have different tastes and that's just it. But what informs our taste?

(Hint: it's "desirability politics.")

When it comes to who we date and who we find attractive, our collective "preferences" as a society are informed by our subconscious bias, our cultural influences, and who we are taught to find attractive through the media and the narratives we consume about the hierarchy of beauty. Which makes every single person's desire and desirability inherently political.

Do you listen to and respect people you're not attracted to?

I sit high on the scale of desirability, being slim, nondisabled, white, cisgender, and feminine. People open up to me and see me as "nice" and "innocent" before I even get a chance to open my mouth. I could be awful, but I am afforded many privileges as a result of being "desirable" by society. Because I am white, I am more likely to be seen and heard. Because my gender expression aligns with society's expectations, I am more likely to be desired. Because I am thin, I have the luxury of being able to dress myself in whatever clothes I like, I don't have to worry about stores not having my size, and I am not questioned about my health choices. Because I am cisgender, people don't question me about my genitals when shopping for clothes the same way they might a trans person. **By existing in the body that I do, I am treated better by society—and that isn't fair.**

It is important to acknowledge that some people are afforded unearned privileges for looking more "desirable" than others. And that while desirability is subject to our individual tastes, society's collective idea of beauty is informed and controlled by the same racist, fatphobic, and sexist beauty standards, and there is a hierarchy.

DON'T CONFLATE FETISHIZATION WITH RESPECT

As you learn to reconnect with the humanity that has been bashed out of your brain since you were younger (no, this isn't going to be a comfortable process), remember not to confuse respecting marginalized people with fetishizing them.

A lot of people, for example, think that if their dating history consists exclusively of Black, fat, trans, or disabled people, or people of color, their dating preferences aren't problematic. But fetishization is as much a problem as avoiding dating certain groups of people. When we fetishize marginalized people, we rid them of their chance to be the unique, multifaceted individuals that they are. Saying "I have a thing for Asian girls"—however well-intentioned—isn't a compliment; you're assuming that "Asian girls" all act as one homogenous group.

> **If we want to take back the control from our subconscious while we navigate the dating world—and shake up the unequal hierarchy that is "desirability"— we have to start by questioning our preferences.**

Each time I date someone new, it's an opportunity to learn about myself as well as this other person. When I use dating apps, I analyze each profile before I swipe left and ask myself, "Why am I not attracted to this person?" It sounds extra, but doing this has helped me to unpack and work through a lot of my unconscious bias that I didn't realize I had, rather than just accepting that "they're not my type." If you get just one takeaway from this book, I want it to be the action of questioning everything. Including yourself.

THIS WAY TO THE SHRINKING MACHINE . . .

In my experience, a lot of my interactions with cis men make me feel like I'm being placed into a shrinking machine. A machine designed to make me just the right amount of desirable, but not too sexy or eye-catching to give him the "wrong idea." Just the right amount of interesting, but not too interesting and not too intelligent, so as to not make him feel emasculated or uncomfortable. It's a pretty exhausting performance and one that women have been doing for centuries. Until we have fully rinsed out the conditioning that women need to shrink themselves around men to accommodate their "masculinity" and take up as little space as possible, we will forever be compromising our multifaceted selves for the sake of their egos.

When I came out as queer, there was an uncomfortable transition I had to undergo, forcibly stepping outside this shrinking machine (dating cis men), so that I could learn how to behave outside of society's archaic gender roles on dates. I wasn't used to living and dating in an uncompromised and unapologetic space. If you've been in the shrinking machine for a while, dating people without performing gender roles, without adhering to heteronormative standards, can feel uncomfortable.

It forces you to see that you always deserved better and that you have lived a life of settling and shrinking. But try to view this discomfort as a growing pain that you have to endure, and find coping mechanisms to push on through. This is good for you. Whether you're transitioning into dating people of different genders or not, any healthy relationship after a toxic one, regardless of gender, can seem quiet and dull when you're used to chaos and danger. Just try to remember that you deserve consistency and communication. You *deserve* this room to breathe and be your multifaceted self.

When you date emotionally unavailable people, some might say you even become addicted to the suffering. The unpredictability can, in fact, psychologically be what drives us to want more of it. It is the human condition to want something more when we don't know the outcome, whether or not we might "win."

How tragic.

We are wired to fall in love with emotionally unavailable people.

GHOSTING

Being ghosted can be one of the most challenging things to overcome when you start dating, because when you're left with no explanation for why wounds have been inflicted, you reflect this inwards. You internalize the rejection, and you see it as a personal fault.

Let's say you had an incredible night with someone who said they'd love to see you again, but they never followed through and didn't text you back. There are a multitude of reasons someone might ghost you—but none of them are about you. Remember what I said about short-term validation? (see page 31.) If you've been ghosted, it's likely that you're the victim of a person who was experiencing low self-worth who was using you as a means of instant gratification. It's likely you were their dopamine "hit." (*Ouch*, I know. I'm sorry.) Or they might have intimacy issues and don't like people to get too close. Or they have an avoidant attachment style. The point being, whatever the reason someone has decided to ghost you, it has nothing to do with your worth. The way people treat you is only ever a reflection of how they feel about themselves, not you. What people don't seem to realize, because of the normalization of ghosting, is how emotionally abusive it can become. Being ghosted causes you to question your self-worth, wondering what you "did wrong" to deserve this. Ghosting should not be a normalized part of your dating experience, as it often takes these subtle forms of emotional abuse.

My advice to someone who has been ghosted? Move on. Do not prolong your suffering. They don't like you.

Don't waste any more energy thinking about this person. No more going over the details with your friends, grasping at straws trying to make excuses for them, or checking up on their socials. If someone likes you, they will make it known. Stop wasting your limited time on this planet wallowing around in "What if?" They're certainly not spending any of their energy thinking about you. They have chosen not to communicate with you, and they didn't close the door, so you're going to have to close it yourself. Unrequited love's a bore. We needn't accept crumbs of validation from unworthy people anymore. We want and deserve the whole damn cake.

DO YOU EVEN WANT TO SEE THIS PERSON AGAIN, OR CAN YOUR EGO JUST NOT HANDLE BEING UNWANTED?

Task: If you don't do it already, I want you to practice giving the closure and communication you expect to receive from others to the people who you are no longer keen on.

There will be a few instances where you need to go no-contact on someone to protect your safety, but outside of that there is almost no reason to avoid communication. Whether that's letting the people you're dating know that you're only looking for something casual, texting a one-night stand to let them know that's as far as you'd like it to go, or communicating to your partner when you feel disrespected instead of becoming passive-aggressive in the hope they "figure it out," so many unpleasant situations can be avoided by just employing direct communication.

People respect people who respect their time—it goes both ways.

Let's close the communication gap.

CHAPTER 10

MAYBE IT'S A GIRL CRUSH; MAYBE YOU'RE A QUEER

Our queer feelings are entirely valid.

Let me start with a bit of clarification, as the words we use and the way we use them matter. It's important to know that the word "queer" has its roots in the history of queer oppression, not empowerment. It originally came into use in the 16th century and meant "strange" or "odd," then began to be used as an insult in the early 19th century towards people who were believed to be in same-sex relationships. However, LGBTQ+ activists in the 1980s reclaimed the word "queer" as a political statement to self-describe their identity.

Today, "queer" is widely used as a term for sexual orientation and gender identities that are not heterosexual or cisgender. If you're not straight, or you don't identify with the same gender you were assigned at birth, you may wish to self-identify as queer. Queer covers all sorts of sexual/gender identities, such as bisexual, asexual, nonbinary, and gender-fluid. It's important to remember that queerness is political.

Equally, some people still remember times when "queer" was used as a slur against them and because of this they don't feel comfortable adopting this label—which is valid too.

Rigid and archaic gender roles got in the way of living my truth for so long. Any time I vocalized my feelings for women and other genders as a closeted bisexual, I was often told that these feelings were just a "fantasy," and a fantasy only for the entertainment of men. On top of this there is a lot of internalized homophobia to work through, which for me sounded in my head like, "You don't look queer enough" or "You've never been with a woman; how do you even know?" But I did know.

I knew because there were times when I'd think about women during sex.

I knew because I had fallen in love with my female friends.

I knew because my thoughts about women were recurring, and the thought of being in a relationship with a woman made me feel at home with myself.

I had always been compelled by women—but I was also attracted to men and people of other genders. So what was it that stopped me from owning my bisexuality?

One night after consuming a lot of cocktails, I ended up crying to my best friend, confessing my feelings for women. I was in a toxic, long-term relationship with a man at the time, and I hadn't allowed the queer in me to breathe. I never saw another person who looked like me dating girls, in the media or in real life, and I thought that people who felt the way I felt and looked the way I looked didn't exist. It's even harder for marginalized people (Black queer people, disabled queer people, etc.) to come to terms with their sexuality, as they're less likely to see themselves represented in the media at all, let alone also represented as queer. But the way you express yourself, how you dress, and your other intersecting identities has no direct correlation with your sexuality. We need to see these things outside of the binary. Who says queer can't be feminine? By invalidating my own queerness, I was stereotyping other queer people. There is no one way to look, present, or act queer.

The stereotypes about the gay community and how being queer is "supposed to look" (i.e., a traditionally masculine gender expression, short hair, etc.) stopped me from embracing an enormous part of my identity, and our society's obsession with heteronormativity (encouragement of heterosexuality and gender roles) is mostly to blame. As a teenager who was having an internal battle between my whole self and what the world, my peers, and family expected of me as a young woman—I hid my feelings for women, put them into a box in my head labeled "Girl Crushes." The term "Girl Crush" was really just my way of saying "no homo." I was deeply embarrassed to admit my feelings for women.

If you're one of those people who talks of having girl crushes or says to their friends, "If I was gay, I'd totally date her," have you ever considered that sexuality exists on a spectrum and that you actually just want to date her?! Bisexuality/pansexuality by definition mean "attraction to more than one gender." I decided in my late teens to unpack the "Girl Crush" box of shame in my head and address that these were just genuine crushes I had on other human beings.

The shame that women have surrounding sex is the same shame that seeps into our desire to be with other genders, because we are taught that our bodies exist and belong to the male gaze—so having feelings for other women is bound to confuse us.

IT'S SOCIETY'S RELUCTANCE TO ACCEPT AND WELCOME QUEER PEOPLE THAT NEEDS TO CHANGE. NOT HOW YOU CHOOSE TO LIVE YOUR LIFE.

For most women, it has been imprinted, stamped, and engraved into our brains that one day we will marry a man and have his children. Heterosexuality is the fairy tale we are spoon-fed growing up. We see it on our TV screens, learn about it in sex ed, and read about it in our bedtime stories. I like to call this relentless bombardment, quite simply, hetrifying. Something so straight and heteronormative that it makes you feel hetrified.

There's a hierarchy of how relationships are viewed in our society, and ones that are comprised of cisgender, white, nondisabled, heterosexual, middle- or upper-class married people with kids are placed on top. But here's the beautiful thing about being queer: by just existing outside of these definitions you get to throw society's restrictive rule book out of the window. You get to write your own damn script—there is far less pressure to adhere to heteronormative ideas of romance, sex, and "relationship progression."

THE FEMALE GAZE

"The influence of heteronormativity and the male gaze was so strong that I, someone who has fallen intensely in love with multiple women, felt like an imposter calling myself bisexual."
—Ramona Marquez

As a bisexual woman, I questioned why it is that I don't enjoy viewing women in the same way that men do; why I don't get instantly turned on from looking at hyper-sexualized images of women. It's because portraying women in this light wasn't created to suit my sexual needs. Women are positioned as sexual objects of desire in the media to feed the appetite of the male gaze (see page 130), and it's toxic to us all. Healthy relationships are not built on objectifying or fetishizing your partner but on respecting them and seeing them as full human beings, not sexual ornaments.

> **The sexualization of women's bodies is so normalized, it made me question whether loving a woman outside of her objectification was valid. That if I didn't objectify women and talk about them the way cis men did, I couldn't possibly be queer. How *hetrifying*.**

Give yourself room to work through your desires and what influences them—what is it about the people you're attracted to that makes you like them? Whether you identify as part of the LGBTQ+ community or not, here are some questions you can use to reflect on your own life, and what role heteronormativity has played in your identity:

- In what ways have the unwritten rules of how your gender "should behave" affected your everyday life, your body language, who you date, your self-expression, and your sex life?
- Do you assume people's sexuality or gender just by looking at them?
- Have you shamed away your queer feelings?

It's society's reluctance to accept and welcome queer people that needs to change—not how we choose to live our lives.

MAYBE IT'S A "GIRL CRUSH"; MAYBE YOU'RE QUEER

CHAPTER 11

LOVE SEX, HATE SEXISM

. . . AND *NEVER* FAKE AN ORGASM

It takes two to tango, so why is a woman's pleasure in heterosexual relationships still so rarely prioritized?

Why are we shamed for even implying that we enjoy sex, that we are able to take pleasure into our own hands through masturbation, or that we have multiple sexual partners the same way cis het men do? What kind of a message does it send to young women if we teach them that only men are supposed to enjoy sex? Are we just supposed to be a mere accessory to their orgasm? Where does our pleasure fit into this? When our sex education is saturated with heteronormativity and lacking in discussion surrounding consent, it's not surprising that so many people are subject to unnecessary trauma during their first time. *Because not one of us knows what the fuck we're doing.*

Sex positivity is about bodily autonomy and your intrinsic right to express your sexuality however you desire. Whether that's by learning what you like and practicing on yourself, meeting someone on Tinder for a commitment-free hookup, or deciding that sex isn't a priority for you at all because you've discovered that you're on the asexual spectrum—all of these are ways of expressing your sexuality. Because guess what? There is no norm.

The way you express your sexuality is valid and is also allowed to change throughout your life. You need only to listen to yourself and your needs in order to discover what sex means for you and what that looks like. Just make sure that you're doing what feels right for you.

LEARN TO ~~LOVE~~ FUCK YOURSELF

I found out how to make myself orgasm from a very young age, and it takes me seconds now. I remember worrying that I'd walk downstairs afterwards and there would be a mark on my face, some kind of "universally acknowledged indicator" that would reveal what I had been up to, and my parents would find out. The guilt was actually so unbearable I once dramatically burst into my mum's room to confess to her that I had "tingly feelings" watching the scene with Rizzo and Kenickie getting it on in the car in *Grease*. The reason I'm sharing my discovery of masturbation with you is because I want to destigmatize it. When I was growing up, I can't even count the amount of times I heard (and believed) from my peers that "girls don't like sex." You hear something repeated enough times, it starts to feel like the truth. When we are taught we "don't like sex," all that teaches us about our sexuality and our bodies is that they are to be reserved exclusively for men and their sexual desires. It normalizes us as "passive participants" in sex and not people who enjoy the experience equally. This narrative is particularly harmful for queer women and often prevents them from coming out until later in life. A lot of queer women have unfulfilling sex with men, but because the normalization of women's discomfort during sex is so deeply internalized,

WHEN I WAS
GROWING UP
I CAN'T EVEN COUNT
THE AMOUNT OF TIMES
I HEARD (AND BELIEVED)
"GIRLS DON'T
LIKE SEX"

they don't realize they're simply not attracted to men. After all, "girls just don't like sex."

It is socially acceptable for boys to watch porn and masturbate, so much so that they can discuss this socially without shame. Can you imagine talking about your "fantastic wank" in front of your friends as a teen without feeling guilt or slut-shame heavy in your chest as you say it?

When we exist in a culture where women are ashamed to talk about their own pleasure, this only further perpetuates the harmful narrative that we don't enjoy sex, because we are too ashamed to talk about it. The first time I spoke about masturbation with my friends felt akin to coming out; it was genuinely liberating and gave me a deep sense of validation, completely abandoning the internal shame I had been harboring for years. It's not always easy to talk about taboo subjects, but once we openly discuss them, the stigma-sting is taken out of them and they become a place of free discussion and exploration.

Not to be dramatic, but my first vibrator changed my motherfucking life.

I bought it a few months after I was sexually assaulted. I didn't want what happened to me to take away the relationship with my body I had spent years rebuilding—I wanted to reclaim my damn pussy, and I wanted to love her again. I was fed up with feeling like she belonged to everyone but herself. Buying this sex toy enabled me to claim back my body for myself. The body I had been shamed into hiding and reserving for men and their gaze for my entire life. I once told an ex-boyfriend about the amazing orgasm I gave myself with a showerhead using *that* setting, and he gave me the silent treatment for an hour. He eventually told me it was because it made him feel useless. Do you see how backwards it is?

That it's "normal" for me to perform sexual acts for his pleasure, but the moment I take control over my own body without a man in the room, I am forced into some kind of "self-reflection treatment" and made to feel shame?

It is imperative that we normalize masturbation for all women. Because if we can normalize masturbation, we also normalize female sexuality and can be viewed as people who deserve to enjoy sex too.

STOP JUDGING PEOPLE ON THEIR SEX LIVES

When it comes to having casual sex, a lot of us have been victims of our internalized misogynist trying to stop us living our best lives while simultaneously slut-shaming other women. But we need to let that shit go. We want to see more women feel as though they are able to command their own lives and choose what's right for them, without feeling an ounce of guilt or shame.

A woman should have the right to choose what she wants for herself, just as men have the right to.

As a queer woman, dating people of different genders made me realize that casual sex can be a shame-free, beautiful, and communicative experience, as opposed to a performance. There's no cis het male gaze present during queer sex (at least, not a physical male gaze present). You can step out of "performance" mode and enter "do whatever the fuck feels good" mode. It's also taught me that encounters without shame do exist. Know that you should never have to settle for anything less than reciprocal, enthusiastic, and

consensual sex. Yes, even if it's casual! This is the bare minimum. *Not only that, it is the law.*

If you have a vulva, buy yourself a hand mirror and promise me you will get to know it. It's frightening how many people have never really seen their own genitals. A lot of the shame we have around pleasuring ourselves, or even prioritizing our orgasms during intercourse, is because we don't even know what they look like, let alone how to work them. One of the most empowering things you can do for yourself is to reconnect with your body and learn about your anatomy. If there's one thing I wish I had had hammered into my skull as a young girl, it's that your body is yours and it belongs to you first and foremost.

If you have a clitoris, get to know it. Neglecting the one part of your body that is designed exclusively to give you pleasure is an intentional effect of years living under patriarchy.

Masturbate as your own private act of resistance.

IF YOU HAVE A
CLITORIS,
GET TO KNOW IT.

CHAPTER 12

IF IT'S NOT A "FUCK YES", IT'S A "NO"

A lot of people are reluctant to ask for consent because they feel like asking "kills the mood." But you know what really kills the mood? Sexually assaulting someone.

Taking a second to consider your partner and check that you're both on the same page shows maturity, high levels of emotional intelligence, and respect for their boundaries. A person who's considerate of their partner's pleasure, who communicates to make sure they're comfortable, exhibits self-awareness. And that means that they're more likely to be aware of their own needs and desires. Self-awareness is, for me, such a turn on. What's hotter than a person who knows what they want and can confidently communicate these desires to their partner? Asking for consent is not only the law, it's very sexy.

Here are a few ways to ask for consent:
- "Do you like that?"
- "Can I take these off?"
- "Is this okay?"
- "Do you mind if we switch positions?"
- "Can I go down on you?"
- "How do you like it?"
- "Are you sure you feel ready for this, or would you prefer if we carried on kissing?"
- "Please know that you can say 'no' at any time."

Consent is mandatory, it is the law, and it's not some form of flirting or foreplay. However, it can seamlessly fit into intercourse. Why not ask to remove their underwear while you're already kissing their neck, or whisper it in their ear? Or ask if they'd like to fuck you between kissing? It doesn't have to be the awkward and robotic script that it's been made out to be (unless that's your thing—we don't kink-shame in this family).

"WE DON'T HAVE TO DO ANYTHING TONIGHT"

As a survivor of sexual assault, nothing makes me feel more comfortable than when the person I'm intimate with creates an environment where I feel like, at any point, I could say "no." When your partner checks in, it takes the onus off you to have to tell them to stop. It relieves you of the pressure to feel like you have to do things you don't want to do.

When you're used to a lifetime of being objectified, for a lot of women nothing feels sexier than safety.

RAPE CULTURE IS MAINTAINED BECAUSE WE FEAR THE CONSEQUENCES OF SIMPLY SAYING "NO" IN THE FIRST PLACE.

This means doing whatever it is you want in the bedroom, knowing that if you wanted it to stop, they would stop. We don't empower women to feel that they're able to reject sexual advances. Rape culture is maintained because we fear the consequences of simply saying "no" in the first place.

We don't empower women to set boundaries. The worst part is that for too many it usually takes a traumatic experience to force them to learn what "boundaries" and "red flags" are in the first place. One of the main reasons I'm writing this book is to introduce these concepts to people, hopefully before they have to learn the hard way like I did.

Many times, people consent to sexual activity because they fear what might happen if they reject someone's advances. But part of dismantling rape culture starts with encouraging women to set and hold boundaries, no matter the reaction they might receive. This is not victim blaming—the responsibility not to rape lies solely with the rapist. But we need to get to a place where women are empowered enough to say "no" in the first place or we will continue to foster a culture of coercion and "blurred lines." Consent is the only way to have sex. If there's no direct exchange of consent, it's rape:

- If you ask for consent and they hesitate or take a little longer to answer, reassure them by saying something like, "It's okay if you don't; would you prefer we just did x instead?"
- If they don't answer with a clear and enthusiastic "yes," it's a "no."
- "I'm tired" doesn't mean "convince me."
- "No" doesn't mean "keep asking until I say 'yes.'"
- "No" is the most definable boundary in the world. There are no "blurred lines" when it comes to consent.

If it's not a "fuck yes," it's a "no."

THE RULES OF SEX

- Ask before doing something or progressing.
- Check in during foreplay.
- Make sure if you want to have intercourse that your partner wants to have it with you too.
- If someone is asleep, unconscious, drunk, or high, they cannot consent to sex.
- Check in with someone every time you start a new sexual activity, whether that's going from oral sex to penetrative sex, or even switching up positions.
- Consenting to sex in the past or being in a relationship with someone does not automatically mean consent for the future. For example, if Sam says he wants to have sex with Sally, but if after 30 minutes of foreplay, Sam says he's too tired, Sally is not then entitled to have sex with Sam because he previously agreed. Sam can change his mind. He does not owe Sally sex.

SEX AND ALCOHOL

Sex is an experience, not a performance.

When it comes to sex, we often feel this need to perform, and we all have our share of body insecurities and self-esteem issues. Whether it's your first time with a new partner or you don't really know what you're doing, it can feel a bit awkward and you might want a drink to take the edge off your anxiety and kick in a bit of confidence. But if you're drinking, remember that drunk consent is not full consent. If you're feeling anxious about wanting to sleep with someone or have low self-esteem when it comes to your body, you should try communicating this with your partner. It might seem scary to open up and be vulnerable, but there is nothing worse than waking up feeling confused and not being able to remember what happened "the night before."

SET SEX BOUNDARIES

We all have different boundaries, but it's important to check in and make sure that you're not slipping into disruptive habits. Here are a few red flags to memorize for the bedroom:

They refuse to wear a condom.

Dump them *immediately*. If someone doesn't respect your body and the consequences you might face for the sake of their temporary burst of pleasure, they've GOT to go. I mean it. If someone removes a condom during sex without your consent, that is sexual assault. There are plenty of people out there who are willing to respect your boundaries—people ignoring your desires and safety is not normal—it's just been normalized.

They're only nice to you during sex or after you've had sex.

They're using you. You're not a person to them; you're an object. Also, if they're only hitting you up late at night, it means you're their quick fix and they only want you when they're bored. Casual sex is totally fine, and you should be able to enjoy it without shame, just like men. But if you feel like deep down you're accepting casual sex from someone when you want a relationship (settling for crumbs when you want the cake, see page 36), then stop settling for it. Someone out there would be honored to have a relationship with you.

They call you demeaning names.
Unless previously agreed that this kind of language is okay with you, if someone starts calling you "slut," "whore," or "bitch" during intercourse, this is a big red flag. Especially if you've asked them to stop and they continue. It shows an enormous lack of respect towards you and your body. Most of this behavior is mimicking tropes found in porn and it's not a sign of an emotionally healthy partner.

They perform any sexual act on you without asking first.
Sure, sex can flow naturally, and we can pay attention to the person's body language to see where things might be going. But consenting to a kiss doesn't mean you're consenting to oral sex. Just because you're having a nice, big sloppy snog on the sofa, it doesn't mean it automatically leads to fingering because "That wAs the VibE." Ask first.

They use guilt and shame.
If someone makes you feel guilty for not having sex or for not liking the same things as them, or uses your insecurities to make you do things you don't want to do? Goodbye.

They expect you to pay for emergency contraception.
Despite both people being equally responsible for protection during sex, people with vaginas are always expected to pay the price for birth control, emergency contraception, and morning-after pills because it's seen as "our problem." This person doesn't care about you enough if they can't share the responsibility.

OTHER FORMS OF CONSENT

The truth is that respecting people's boundaries goes beyond sex. An ex-boyfriend once drew on my body and took pictures of me while I was sleeping. Men physically put their hands on my waist to move me out of their way, instead of politely asking me to move. Women come up to me in the bathroom and off-load their trauma, expecting me to offer free therapy.

Our relationship with boundaries, whether setting our own or respecting other people's, depends on our upbringing and reenacting our earliest relationships from childhood out of our subconscious. While this may explain someone's lack of boundaries, it does not excuse them. We must actively work to rewrite what we know to develop healthier boundaries, so we're able to maintain better relationships with others and ourselves.

Here are some ways we violate boundaries:
- Asking someone to do something more than once, after they've already said "no." By doing this, they push the person into feeling pressured to compromise their boundaries to please someone else.
- Entering someone's bedroom without permission (depending on the relationship).
- Taking pictures of people without consent (when someone is sleeping, walking down the street, and so on).
- Borrowing people's things without asking first.
- Reading people's phones without their consent.
- Touching people's hair without consent.
- Off-loading your problems onto friends, strangers, or people on the internet without checking in first.
- Helping someone without asking if they want help.
- Giving unsolicited advice to someone who never asked for it.

- Pursuing someone who has given adequate signals that they're not interested or that the relationship has ended.
- Outing someone as LGBTQ+.

Having a lack of boundaries doesn't just mean we're more susceptible to accept things that aren't good for us; it also means we're likely to exhibit toxic behaviors ourselves that could cause harm to someone else.

Here are some signs that you have unhealthy boundaries:
- You touch other people without asking.
- You go against your own personal beliefs and values to please other people. For example, taking drugs on a night out because everyone else is doing it, even though you don't usually do them.
- You fall in love with someone new very quickly. It's a sign that you're seeking validation and need something to make you feel whole. You can't love someone you know nothing about.
- You off-load your life story and your traumas to someone when you first meet them.
- You find it hard to say "no."
- You give as much as you can for the sake of giving, without asking for reciprocity.
- You subconsciously seek partners who need fixing and healing.
- You constantly excuse someone's mistreatment of you—i.e., "They're only like this when they're drunk."
- You protect people who are doing damage to you.

I had to end a toxic relationship when I realized the treatment I had allowed and accepted from someone meant that my boundaries had become nonexistent. I had allowed my boundaries to be worn down over years to accept a love that was less than I deserved.

The ultimate act of self-love is to know when to walk away from a toxic relationship. Though hard, this is actively practicing self-care, self-preservation, and self-worth.

It's never too late to recognize your own shortcomings and set boundaries with people in your life.

Love yourself enough to walk away.

CHAPTER 13

"WHAT DID SHE EXPECT, GOING OUT LIKE THAT?"

Experiencing discomfort, fear, or aggression during intercourse should not be normalized.

Maybe one day I'll "tell my story," but I don't think details are important. For now, I'll just say "me too" and use this space in my book to pass on the lessons I had to learn the hard way. However, I'm afraid there's one thing I can't teach you—I can't teach you how to avoid sexual assault. It's not something anyone can avoid by taking protective measures, because sexual assault is never your fault.

Having "uncomfortable sex" is, unfortunately, seen as sort of a necessary introduction to womanhood. This cultural idea that "girls don't enjoy sex" makes our uncomfortable experiences feel normal—it normalizes and justifies rape. This is what we mean by "rape culture." Here are some features of our current rape culture:

- Common idioms such as "boys will be boys" that excuse men's actions, and popular songs that insinuate that there are "blurred lines" when it comes to consent with lyrics like "I know you want it."
- Using rape jokes as a form of male bonding.
- America electing a president who bragged about using his position of power to commit sexual assault and "grabbing women by the pussy."
- Encouraging women to take to preventative measures to "avoid" being raped instead of taking measures to stop people from raping in the first place. These include "covering up," buying rape whistles, never walking home alone, moving to an apartment where you can see who's at the door before they can see you, carrying keys between your fingers, not making eye contact with men, packing an extra layer for the walk home, lying about where you live, choosing shoes in case you need to run, avoiding jewelry that makes a noise and draws attention, deciding who you give your number to, making sure there's something in your purse to fight off an attacker.
- Rapists rarely ever seeing a prison cell. Only 0.5 percent of sexual assaults in the U.S. result in any jail or prison time for the perpetrator.[1]

There's a world of silence that quietly and insidiously enables the system of sexual violence to continue. However, cracks are beginning to show. Through #MeToo, more victims are speaking up. Slowly our secret, disgusting reality is being revealed. An apocalypse would occur if every single person guilty of rape and sexual assault was outed—people would not know how to cope with the realization that so many they know and love have been

1   "The Criminal Justice System: Statistics." RAINN. Accessed April 8, 2020. https://www.rainn.org/statistics/criminal-justice-system.

complicit in sexual violence, especially since rape is so normalized some people don't even realize they themselves have committed it.

In order for things to change, there needs to be an open conversation about what has happened, how we can stop it from happening again, and making it clear to everyone from a young age what does and doesn't constitute consent. When something like sexual violence is normalized, it forces its victim to question if what happened to them is a big enough deal to speak out against. But it is a big deal. Sexual assault is always a big deal.

ONE OF THE "NICE GUYS," HUH?

Rape culture spins the narrative that "nice guys" don't rape. But they do. In fact, 80 percent of all rape perpetrators are already known to the victim.[2] These "monsters" we imagine and spend our entire lives being taught to avoid in the streets and in dark alleyways are actually already in our lives. They have sisters, mothers, friends, careers, families—you might even share a bed with them. This harmful narrative—that the only rapists are unknown "monsters" preying on strangers—is an enormous component of rape culture and puts the onus back on the victim to take every precaution to "prevent" rape happening to them.

SOME THINGS AREN'T NORMAL; THEY HAVE BEEN NORMALIZED. THERE'S A DIFFERENCE.

When we have said that we're "too tired"; when we have asked them to "stop"; when we haven't given communicative consent. It's easy to blame rape culture on the fact that consent is only recently being discussed in

2 "Perpetrators of Sexual Violence: Statistics." RAINN. Accessed April 8, 2020. https://rainn.org/ statistics/perpetrators-sexual-violence?_ga=2.24688058.183190519.1586365206-648286353. 1586365206.

some schools, but what kind of a person still wants to have sex with someone who has verbally or physically expressed disinterest, someone who looks uncomfortable, or someone who is scared? Yes, consent is not taught in many schools, but there is a lack of empathy and respect present that would allow someone to enjoy a sexual encounter with an unenthusiastic partner. The problem is also deeply entrenched because of the extreme and violent types of porn that are widely available to (not to mention produced by and for) men. We live in a culture that breeds and encourages toxic masculinity at the expense of women and our bodies. But I'm bored of blaming the "culture" that rapists were raised in. We forget that people create culture—and it's time to hold these people accountable for their actions.

STOP INTERROGATING RAPE VICTIMS

If someone talks to you about their experience of rape or sexual assault, never ask them why they didn't report it. Never ask them why they're not fighting it. Treat people as experts on their own experiences and believe them.

Sexual assault is the only crime where we interrogate the victim as though they were the perpetrator. You wouldn't ask someone who was robbed, "Why didn't you fight the attacker off?" because as a society we understand and respect that other people's personal possessions are not for others to take without consent. Duh! But when it comes to sexual assault, some still believe that women's bodies exist solely for consumption. If she's walking home late at night? It's up for grabs. Think about that for a second. We respect other people's wallets and material possessions, and treat reports of theft more seriously than we do the rape of women's bodies.

Things to avoid saying to a victim of sexual assault:
- "Did you definitely say 'no'?"
- "What were you wearing?"
- "Did you try to fight them off?"
- "Why haven't you reported it? They can't get away with this."
- "Be careful about reporting it; you could ruin their career."
- "Are you sure it was rape?"
- "Did they definitely hear you say 'no'?"
- "Somebody really wanted to have sex with you?"

Affirming things to say to a victim of sexual assault:
- "Thank you for trusting me with your story."
- "I believe you."
- "How can I support you?"
- "However you handle this situation, I support your decision."
- "You didn't deserve this."

People are so quick to ask survivors why we didn't report it, without realizing there are systems and people every step of the way to ensure this never happens—even when we do try to seek justice. The system fails so many rape victims every single day. Rape is the most underreported crime, and, after my experience, I finally understood why. I told a person of authority the day after it happened, and they encouraged me not to report it: "I'd think twice; this might ruin his career."

Months later, I decided I would ignore this advice, and I got up the courage to report it anyway. I went to a sexual assault clinic to talk to the police, and

they told me there was "nothing they could do" and that there would be "no point" in reporting it.

So, I'm writing to you to be the person I needed in that moment. To remind you that if you're worried the truth might "destroy a man's career"—fuck his career. That's on him—he should have thought about that before he took what didn't belong to him.

Go ahead. I believe you.

WOMEN DO NOT EXIST TO SATISFY THE MALE GAZE

"A man in a room full of women is ecstatic.
A woman in a room full of men is terrified."
—Unknown

It costs more to be a woman in the same world where we are paid substantially less than men, and we're supposed to believe that "splitting the bill" is the route to equality? Regardless of your gender, this should make your blood boil. This eye-opening perspective on patriarchy was first introduced to me by author and activist Chidera Eggerue, and I haven't stopped thinking about it since.

Here are just a few examples of the tax we end up paying for misogyny, and how the presence of the heterosexual male gaze limits our experience in this society:

- We choose our route home based not on efficiency, but on which route is less likely to have men lurking around who will potentially harass or assault us.
- We give a fake name and number to a guy who won't leave us alone in a bar or say that we have a boyfriend, because we fear what he might do if we just say "no."
- The money we spend on preventative measures "just in case"—rape whistles, pepper spray, Tasers.
- The money we spend on contraceptive measures and morning-after pills.
- Queer women are not able to show displays of affection in public because of the sexualized response from men and the unwanted attention it attracts. Girl-on-girl love in public is always assumed to be a "performance" for men.
- Constant vigilance and awareness of our every move in public, to avoid giving men "the wrong idea."
- The resources of time, energy, and money that go into being "presentable" (aka "desirable" by racist, fatphobic, transphobic beauty standards) so that we are met with basic human respect.
- The money we spend on cars and taxis to get home safely, when men and people with male-passing privilege have the option to just walk home or take the bus because they don't fear being attacked or raped.
- If we do decide to walk home, we often pack an extra layer or an entirely different outfit to wear to and from the club/bar.
- Any applied effort to our appearance as women is considered an "invitation" for men to start talking to us, so we often dress ourselves

down or cover ourselves up to avoid receiving unsolicited remarks. Even then, if this isn't effective, we police our body language.

- The male gaze has sexualized and objectified our bodies so much that they have been shamed of their inherent use: to function. People who have periods hide sanitary products and feel ashamed of our periods when we need to go to the bathroom.
- Getting off public transportation early because we have been harassed/made to feel uncomfortable, as the threat of someone following us home if we get off at our actual destination is very real.
- The embarrassment/shame of breastfeeding in public.

The consequences of the male gaze are exhausting and expensive. We spend money and energy keeping ourselves safe from men, and yet still—*we are paid less than them.*

"The male gaze" is a term coined by Laura Mulvey to describe the way women are portrayed as objects in the media. It has insidiously permeated every facet of our lives and identities.

Everyday rituals—applying makeup, shaving, doing our hair, and choosing our clothes—are all decisions subconsciously filtered through the desires of the all-powerful male gaze. These are the rituals that we are expected to perform in order to be treated with the same respect men are afforded for showing up just as they are.

BODY POLITICS

What kind of a relationship are we expected to have with our own bodies when we are socialized to believe that they exist for male consumption? We are taught that men are entitled to our bodies so much so that we are blamed for being assaulted because of our choice of clothing but still expected to present ourselves in a way that is desirable enough for their validation and basic respect. The mixed messages we receive about our

EVERYDAY BEAUTY
RITUALS ARE
SUBCONCIOUSLY
FILTERED THROUGH
THE DESIRES
OF THE MALE
GAZE

bodies make us incredibly vulnerable to capitalism, as we are encouraged to buy solutions to fix our biological "flaws." The shame surrounding body hair on women, for example, was a seed planted by male advertisers in 1915, because they realized they could make money selling razors to women. Before then, women weren't expected to shave—there was no stigma around not shaving our body hair. But they planted the seed of insecurity to create a new market for their products. Voilà! We're now trained and socialized to be disgusted by our own bodies in order to cater to male consumption and capitalist profit.

THE MALE GAZE ACTIVELY LIMITS AND RESTRICTS YOUR EXPERIENCE ON THIS PLANET.

The limitation that the male gaze has imposed on my life is one of the main reasons that I go to therapy. It manifests as anxiety that cramps my stomach and makes me short of breath when I walk down the street at night, and at times during the day too, and fear for my safety when I'm on a date with another woman. When you're on a queer date there's no "seizing the moment" that you get on hetero dates. When it comes to kissing or any form of affection, you scan the room for lurking eyes, and have to check that it's a safe place for you and the person you're with.

Being visibly queer in the UK, where I live, isn't as safe as the media would have you believe, and when you're two queer girls on a date, you'll often be approached by men who think you're just friends. After all, what could two girls possibly be doing at a bar, if not looking for male attention? I have literally been holding the hand of a girl at a bar and had a man come over trying to chat her up, and when I told him we were on a date, he went, "Don't worry, that's hot! I'm into that!"

I swear to God—you cut men and they bleed audacity.

HOW MUCH OF MY FEMININITY IS WHO I TRULY AM, AND HOW MUCH OF IT IS A PRODUCT OF PATRIARCHAL BRAINWASHING TO EXIST FOR MALE CONSUMPTION?

When I think about who *Florence Given* really is, I imagine that she's locked deep inside of me, hidden, waiting to be revealed. She's feeling suffocated, wrapped inside the false narratives that have told her who she should be.

I can't help but wonder how much of my identity is a product of this conditioning. How are we ever supposed to know who we really are if we have been brainwashed since birth to identify with the limitations and restrictions inherent in our assigned binary gender? How are we supposed to know how much of our identity is constructed or real; how much of it is a product of the society we were brought up in?

The ways our decisions are controlled by the male gaze are so insidious we don't even realize that it affects the choices we make on a daily basis. There are so many ways that we bear the consequences of patriarchy, and what's frustrating is that we are expected to show up in a way that pleases men just to exist in this world and to be treated with the respect we deserve. This costs money. Capitalism turns us all into objects of desire yet also expects us to pay the price to fit into this accepted vision. Never are we asked about how we want to look for our own visual satisfaction. As long as we don't question the status quo and continue not to challenge the ways patriarchy affects our lives, we prolong our suffering.

If you ever discover parts of yourself that make you feel electric in a world that feeds off your insecurities, please cherish them. Be proud, for they are the parts of yourself that blossomed and survived despite years of assimilation. These are your best bits, your authentic self.

CENSORED

One of the most confusing messages we receive about our bodies is that we are told our worth is tied to our ability to be sexy and desirable, that our bodies are tools to be used to sell products to generate profit for companies—but once we are seen to be harnessing that power for ourselves, once we are seen taking control of our own sexuality, we are a threat. A woman who has no shame around her sexuality, who knows her own power and is capable of harnessing her objectification for her own financial gain or self-empowerment, is a threat to capitalism and the status quo. She's also an absolute fucking icon.

Enter the all-powerful and insidious tool of violence: shame.

Shame does not want you to have autonomy over your own body, because society relies on having control over your body as its product—and products aren't supposed to feel "empowered." Shame is the tool that stops you from exploring self-pleasure and masturbation, because it means you might realize you don't need men for sex. Shame exists in the form of calling women "bitchy" to make us feel embarrassed for speaking up and setting boundaries, keeping us vulnerable and easier to manipulate. Shame exists in the form of censoring women's nipples. (Not all nipples, of course! Just female nipples.) Shame is weaponized to sap your self-worth. The world does not want you to wake up to the fact it is profiting from your subjugation, shame, and insecurities. It doesn't want you to tap into your inherent power.

Inner observation task: Think about something you've always wanted to experiment with in your appearance, and ask yourself why you've never done it.

What parts of your self-expression feel like a routine?
What parts of the way you express yourself feel electric?

In what ways have you internalized the male gaze in your standards of beauty and sexualized women's bodies?

For example, I'd spent the majority of my adolescence wearing skintight clothing because I'd internalized the message that women are to be trophy-esque figures of desirability. My friends and I wore uncomfortable body-con dresses we couldn't sit down in, paired with painfully high heels, to parties. We taped our tits up to make them look bigger, wore shapewear under our dresses so we didn't have to spend the whole evening holding in our stomachs, and we had cuts on our legs from shaving close enough to remove every last prickle. I was doing all this and battling an eating disorder at fourteen years old. I was taught that for women to be seen as desirable, we must experience discomfort. The phrase "beauty is pain" stuck with me—and it hurt me.

As soon as I came out as bisexual to my friends and family, I felt like I finally had room to breathe. To question *everything*.

I asked myself for the first time who the hell I was even doing this painful performance for. Was I "doing it for me" or was I doing it to be validated by the male gaze? The answer: both.

The influence of the male gaze was so strong I had mistaken it for my own idea of beauty. Shortly after I acknowledged this, I allowed myself to wear more baggy clothing, and I started to feel electric in my gender expression. I felt both sexy and comfortable, something I didn't even know was possible.

I feel electric when I wear a suit, but I feel equally euphoric wearing nothing but a pair of leopard-print platforms. The difference is that now I view my gender expression as something that is constantly refining itself, finding ways to connect back to who I was before I was told to be someone else.

Think about what makes you feel alive in your body and jot down those moments as they arise in your life.

Outer observation task: The next time you watch a film, pay attention to how the female characters are positioned. Is the focus on the woman all about her desirability and curves? Does she even have much to say, or are all the important lines given to the male actors? Does her character reinforce sexist stereotypes about women? Does she "risk everything for love" and only talk about relationships? The Bechdel Test was created in 1985 by author Alison Bechdel, and it has three criteria: (1) the movie has to have at least two women in it, who (2) talk to each other, about (3) something besides a man. You'll be surprised at how few movies pass it.

If you want to see the double standard of how men and women are expected to show up in the world, just watch the dynamics of an awards show. You'll see a woman with three people holding up her dress just to get onstage, and targeted ads on Instagram trying to sell you diet tea so you can attain her "event-ready figure" when in reality it took a team of people to wrap her in plastic wrap just to get her into her corset. Meanwhile, male attendees get to show up reasonably well-groomed in a standard tux and tie, no heroic efforts required.

After all, men are invited to these events to win a trophy—not be one.

WHICH PARTS OF YOUR SELF-EXPRESSION FEEL LIKE A ROUTINE, AND WHICH PARTS MAKE YOU FEEL ELECTRIC?

CHAPTER 15

STOP PUTTING PEOPLE ON A PEDESTAL

"A pedestal is as much a prison as any small, confined space."
—Gloria Steinem

We cannot fall in love with the idea that we have created of someone and then feel disappointed when they don't turn out to be the person we invented. This disappointment isn't justified. We're not entitled to feel let down by someone for not matching the fictitious narrative we have written about them and projected from our own mind.

When we think of projection, we usually associate it with projecting our insecurities onto other people. However, projection can also manifest as inappropriate idolization of people who highlight something we feel we are lacking within ourselves.

Putting someone on a pedestal dehumanizes them. With the expectation of perfection comes inevitable disappointment.

The person who has been placed on a pedestal feels pressure to perform and act in a certain way to avoid letting you down. They may fear you won't love them if you "knew the real them," or if they dared to be vulnerable and let down their guard in front of you. By placing someone on a pedestal, you actually prevent yourself from forming a meaningful relationship with them.

There's a difference between putting someone on a pedestal and holding them in high regard.

When you put someone on a pedestal, you place yourself below them and project onto them the parts of yourself that you feel you lack. You may compromise your own beliefs and boundaries to keep them in your life or to please them.

We often secretly believe that "greatness" exists outside of ourselves, unable to acknowledge and nurture our own talents. We try to avoid the uncomfortable truth that we don't actually know ourselves or what we want from life. Emulating our role models is one thing, but living our lives in a way we believe they would approve of when that goes against our own values and beliefs is another.

HOW TO TAKE SOMEONE OFF A PEDESTAL

If you realize that you're putting someone above yourself, it's an indication that you need to do some digging and figure out what it is you feel you're lacking. If someone's presence makes you feel insecure or brings out an ugly jealousness in you, your inner child is asking to be looked after and nurtured. So tend to them.

- Practice the self-love rituals on page 195. You must build a stronger sense of self and your own identity. We imitate people who appear to have the levels of beauty, self-awareness, creativity, and confidence we aspire to, but how are we ever supposed to know who we really are if we're constantly living in someone else's shadow? No one's imaginary approval is ever worth compromising your own boundaries and beliefs for.
- Think about what makes you come alive and what ignites a fire inside of you—*and do more of that.* Follow that feeling. When you're used to defining your success against another's, you can lose sight of what it is you actually want to achieve in life. *This is why you are stagnant!* What makes another person feel happy and fulfilled won't necessarily do the same for you.
- Realize that the person you're pedestalling probably has their own person on a pedestal above them too. Wild, right? Because they're human, flawed, and full of projections and insecurities, just like you.
- Realize that people don't owe you *shit.* People don't owe you "nice" and people don't owe it to you to perform the parts of themselves that you fell in love with. The world owes you nothing, and equally, you owe it nothing. Remember these words to keep your ego in check every now and then.

Burn your idols; take them off the pedestal. And, please, if I'm on your pedestal, in the words of Roxane Gay, "consider me already knocked off."

You're not in love with your idols—they are just mirroring the greatness that already exists within you.

NO ONE'S APPROVAL IS EVER WORTH **COMPROMISING** YOUR OWN BOUNDARIES AND ABANDONING YOUR OWN BELIEFS.

CHAPTER 16

LIFE'S SHORT— DUMP THEM

Dump them. Why? Because you always deserve better.

Every day, I receive hundreds of messages asking for relationship advice. But I never reply to a single one of them. The answer is, and always will be, the same.

Because life is too short to remain in an unfulfilling relationship for the sake of staying in your comfort zone. Your new life is waiting for you. Stop shrinking yourself, shed your old skin, and watch how you blossom and evolve. Watch how you become an even more refined version of the already incredible person you are, outside of a relationship where you're encouraged to view yourself as someone's "other half." Sometimes the dead bits we cut off to encourage growth are our split ends—and sometimes it's a whole husband.

If you have to ask whether or not you should stay with someone who leaves your messages on read, leaves a mess around the house for you to clean up, or has a tendency to lie—you already know the answer. While breaking up with someone who has a history of toxic behavior may seem like the obvious thing to do, so many people stay in these relationships because they don't believe there's going to be another love after this one, and they just don't believe that they deserve better. There's something that forms in abusive relationships called a "trauma bond," where over time we learn to associate romantic love with compromising. I was that person. I didn't have anyone in my life telling me that I deserved better. I had no one telling me that, while I was settling for crumbs, someone out there wanted to give me the whole damn cake. I intentionally avoided and dismissed content with #DumpHim messaging when I was in a bad relationship because I knew I would be faced with the truth that I was settling. In the words of Chidera Eggerue, whose relentless campaigning against settling for shit men inspired me to be vocal about my own experiences, I was "actively ignoring this advice to my own detriment."

No one likes to be told they deserve better, because it means acknowledging that you have to change. But you are allowed to unapologetically want more for yourself. Give yourself that permission.

A lot of people stay in relationships out of fear of being single. But here's the beautiful thing about being single—take a second to think about how incredibly unique and wonderful you are already. Think about all of your interests and passions, your music taste, the clothes you wear; think of all the parts that make up the unique person you are. By choosing to focus on yourself and choosing to be intentionally single, you are only going to become a more refined version of yourself. A whole, refined, evolving bitch. By being single, you are only going to become more of the person the world has kept you from becoming by conditioning you to fit into its boring, binary system. The glow-up that ensues after a good dumping is so hideously fantastic, you won't even recognize yourself.

There's nothing to be afraid of—walk into your own arms.

STOP RAISING HIM; HE'S NOT YOUR SON

Do you find yourself pouring endless amounts of energy into your partner, in the hope that he will grow into the person you want him to be?

Does it ever feel like you've adopted a child in a man's body?

Does your relationship feel draining?

Do you book his appointments?

Do you make sure he gets to places on time?

Do you clean up after him?

Are you his mom?

No? So stop raising him.

While my message of not settling for less than you deserve does apply to any couple regardless of gender, I decided to intentionally add my voice to the existing #DumpHim movement, because there is a very specific type of settling that happens in heterosexual relationships. As women, we are socialized to be "nurturers" and caregivers, and we often end up dating men who fill the role of the person receiving that care. We have been told our whole lives that relationships are about compromise, but you should never have to compromise yourself. There are people in the world who would kill to spend an evening in a restaurant in your presence, but you're too busy seeing the "potential" in your boyfriend, who refuses to get a job because he thinks his band (which hasn't played a single gig yet) is going to single-handedly "change the music industry"? There are people out there who are willing to respect your boundaries and engage in a reciprocal relationship, but you're too busy booking your boyfriend's doctor appointments, doing his laundry, and covering his rent? Women are not rehabilitation centers for men who have yet to reach their final form.

You are not his mom.
You are not his therapist.
You do not owe anyone that energy.
You owe that shit to *yourself*.

Want to know what the final straw with my ex was that finally made me dump him? He called me a bitch. Much worse things had happened in our relationship, but in that moment, something just clicked. I realized that if my unconscious self-neglect had reached the point where bad behavior had become so normalized that someone who supposedly loved me had the audacity to comfortably and carelessly call me a bitch, I owed a lot of TLC and rehabilitation to myself. That word managed to penetrate the thick surface of the bubble I'd been living in for the last three years and successfully burst it.

Don't ever value your relationship on how much shit you can take from someone. Heteronormativity, movies, novels, your parents, and even your friends will have you believing that you're "strong" for "putting up with a man's shit." Lord. Can you hear it now? Please tell me you can hear how absurd this notion is! Your ability to take shit from a man and "stick by his side" says nothing about how strong you are. It does, however, say everything about your low self-esteem and how much of a people-pleasing pushover you've been manipulated into becoming. You have learned to betray yourself and compromise the things you desire and believe in for the validation that you are desired by someone.

People who do not add any value to your life deserve no place in it. Simple. If you're lowering your standards to let someone into your life, dump them. Lowering your standards means that you're compromising your boundaries. Boundaries should never be compromised; they are your own personal law. Anyone who crosses them after you have explicitly made them known has broken your law and needs to be banished from the access of knowing you. People will call you intimidating, bossy, make you believe that you have set your standards too high, and you might start to believe them. Don't. Your phone may be dry for a few months; you might not go on a successful date with someone for over a year. But, honestly, who cares? Buy a sex toy! Wouldn't you rather spend that time focusing on your career, nurturing your mental health, and preserving your beautiful energy? Rather than waste it on someone who makes you feel like you need to shrink yourself in exchange for their crumbs? Ignoring red flags will only come back to bite you in the ass later!

You deserve better, and the annoying thing is that you already know this.

DATING RED FLAGS

Here are five signs that you're compromising yourself and your boundaries, and that you should DUMP THEM.

If you feel like you're compromising your politics by being with this person, dump them.

Trying to change someone's entire political belief system is far too much unpaid labor and totally not worth it. There are nearly eight billion people on this planet, and no matter your sexuality, there's someone out there who holds the same beliefs as you. I know that sometimes it can feel like it's our responsibility to educate people (especially if they're bigots), but it is not your responsibility to help "grow" or "change" these people. It's also impossible.

If you feel like you have to "tone down" or compromise your style for someone, dump them.

If any part of your identity at all is being squashed, suppressed, or erased, they're not the one for you. There's someone out there who is so ready to love you and accept every gorgeous facet of your identity. (Hint: it's you.)

If you find that you're always withholding your good news from someone, or you feel like you need to undermine your achievements to make them comfortable, dump them.

Don't fuck with people who have such a fragile sense of self that your achievements make them uncomfortable. Good luck to them! I hope they heal their wounds, but it's not your job to do it for them. Dump them.

If you have to say "no" more than once because they ignored you the first time, "didn't hear you," or coerced you into something you originally said you didn't want to do, dump them.

There are no blurred lines when it comes to enthusiastic consent. If they do not respect your boundaries, they do not respect you. This goes beyond sex. Someone who chooses to ignore you when you say "no" to anything is bad news.

If they make you feel like you need to shrink yourself, if they belittle your achievements, mock or attack the things you care about, dump them.

An ex of mine would constantly belittle my music taste, and I think he did it to assert power—making him feel in control by feeling superior. Now I get to dance around in my underwear, uncompromised, to whatever the hell kind of music I want. Bliss.

If you find yourself constantly making excuses for or lying about your partner's behavior to your friends and family, dump them. When we hide the details from people it's because we know we will have to be accountable and make changes.

Alternatively, if you find you yourself doing any of these to your partner or someone you're dating, then you're probably not ready for a relationship. Until those parts of yourself are healed, either through deep self-reflection or, ideally, therapy, you will repeat the pattern over and over, expecting different results. But for different results there needs to be an internal shift. You must not seek wholeness and validation in others and relationships; it's unfair to expect them to take on the labor of fixing you while being on the receiving end of emotional abuse.

Stop putting up with things you don't have to put up with. Surround yourself only with what makes you happy—everything else must go.

What is a relationship's purpose in your life if it does not bring you joy?

CHAPTER 17

YOU DON'T HAVE TO GET MARRIED

(NO, REALLY)

I am not against marriage. But . . .

I am all for people doing whatever the hell they want as long as it doesn't harm someone in the process. And if that happens to involve getting married, then I'm happy for those who choose to walk down that aisle. However, no matter how hard the world has tried, the institution of marriage has never been something I've felt I needed to complete my life for the following reasons:

- Imagine getting the government involved once you've fallen in love with someone to make sure they don't leave.
- Imagine also needing permission from the government to leave that relationship.
- Imagine having to ask your father's permission for you to be owned by someone else.
- Imagine your father "giving you away" as you walk down the aisle— like cattle, from one owner to the next, ready to be branded with your new owner's surname.

- Imagine your father viewing this exchange as a beautiful tradition and one of his "lifelong goals."
- Imagine feeling like you have to stay with someone because you are contracted to stay with them for the rest of your life.
- Imagine partaking in a ceremony that has historically excluded LGBTQ+ people and interracial relationships.
- Imagine being trans, and your wife/husband/partner being able to legally veto your right to transition.

Marriage is deeply entrenched in archaic patriarchal tradition and has its roots in an abusive, oppressive history—the ownership of women.

Heteronormativity has truly fucked us all up so much, to the point that we have widely accepted marriage as the pinnacle of great romance (so much so that we feel offended when our partner takes "too long" to propose!). The point of marriage has always been to own women and their bodies. Until 1991, you could legally rape your wife in the UK. Once she uttered the words "I do" at the altar, it meant that you could do what you pleased with her because, with the permission of her father, she was now your property and no longer his. The rape of an unmarried woman used to be viewed as a property crime against her father, robbing him of his daughter's virginity. In some cases, the woman was forced to marry her rapist. The rape of a married woman by a man other than her husband was construed as a crime against her husband, with no concern for the woman herself. Marriage was (and still is in some countries) seen as a contract of ownership.

THE "SECOND SHIFT"

When working women in heterosexual marriages come home from their jobs, they often prepare for their second shift.

Women have been working for free since the beginning of time. We might not realize it, but acknowledging that this explains why I have felt so exhausted in past relationships has liberated me and enabled me to set boundaries around my emotional intelligence and abundant empathy, something I give so freely to everyone but myself.

"Women are just better at that stuff!"

Women's unpaid contributions to the well-being of their homes, partners, and children are overlooked and attributed to the "fact" that women are just natural-born caregivers. We are socialized to be more self-aware and in touch with our emotions, and we are then expected to be caregivers because of it.

The antiquated gender roles of our society still expect women to do the majority of domestic work. They haven't yet caught up with the fact that most of us are now also working full-time jobs. As a result, we're fucking exhausted. We don't ever switch off. But because the impact of household labor isn't easily quantifiable, we are rarely rewarded or compensated for our time and energy. It becomes expected rather than gratefully accepted. In fact, a lot of narratives we see about married women praise them for self-sacrifice. How often do you hear that used in narratives about men?

Married men rarely need to "make time for themselves" because their wives are doing it *for* them, behind the scenes.

I often think about what would happen if, for just one day, women everywhere refused to overextend themselves. I truly believe the world as we know it would crumble. Remembering people's birthdays, cleaning clothes, cooking, tidying up after others, anticipating others' needs, being polite to men who

make us uncomfortable, doing our makeup
in the mornings and skincare routine before bed,
offering our help without any real acknowledgment for it.
Women are often in positions where they have to constantly remind
others to take care of themselves, neglecting themselves in the process.
*This is why self-care is uniquely important for women and marginalized
genders.*

At the time of writing, I am twenty-one years old and have only
been in one long-term relationship with a man. I lived with him for a
month and, despite not being married, I found myself slipping into the
role of housewife. He'd return from work and I'd ask him to pick up his
things that he'd strewn across the floor, and he'd say, "I've been at work
all day; I'm exhausted," as if I hadn't been working all day too. Sharing
the workload of chores was nonexistent; it was an act of labor even asking
him to help. One day, he came home, opened the cupboards, and said,
"Why is there no food? I'm hungry." It was then that I realized I had
become his caretaker, not his partner.

THE NARRATIVE™

We have been indoctrinated to romanticize weddings, and our cultural
obsession with The Narrative™ (aka husband, house, kids) distracts
women from the often oppressive truth of marriage using its usual
capitalist methods—the illusory haze of a shiny engagement ring and the
promise that once we are married, we will finally be living our perfect
life. We're taught that it is only by living The Narrative™ that we will
feel complete, that we will have succeeded because we have achieved
our purpose.

I think it's important to acknowledge that for some people, not
getting married isn't an option. People marry for all sorts of reasons
outside of love; it's also been a long-fought battle for LGBT people

to be able to adopt children in a society that demands marriage be a part of that process. We can't ignore that society rewards us with certain privileges the closer we hew to its narratives. Aside from not having your life decisions questioned constantly, being married rewards you with significant tax perks too.

A woman is so much more than her relationship status. It's literally the least interesting thing about her. Something I've practiced with my friends in an attempt to reverse years of heteronormative brainwashing is refraining from asking them about their love life when we are having a catch-up. If they bring it up, they bring it up. But by immediately asking our friends, "Sooooo, are you seeing anyone at the moment? Tell me all the details!" we emphasize the importance of romantic relationships in our lives and reinforce that we are defined by our relationship status. What if they're not seeing anyone? Will you be just as excited for them then? Ask them about what they've been up to instead, how their job's going, or if they have any exciting projects coming up. If we want people to live happy and fulfilled lives regardless of their relationship status, we can start by deprioritizing the topic of our love lives in our conversations.

Ask yourself if marriage is something you've "always wanted to do." Or if it's something you've always been *told* you wanted to do.

CHAPTER 18

STOP ASSUMING

To assume makes an ass of you and me.
Don't assume someone's ethnicity.
Don't assume someone's ability.
Don't assume someone's gender.
Don't assume someone's sexuality.
Don't assume someone's pronouns.
Don't assume someone's background.
Don't assume shit.
Full stop.

GENDER

It's in our nature to assume things of people. We pick up certain pieces of information from their appearance and body language and make a quick assessment based on how they present themselves and how they act around us. It helps us make sense of the world. But we must learn to take these identity indicators as just that. *A first assessment.*

We're raised from birth to exist within binaries—male or female—and each has their own rigid, archaic gender roles associated. Most of us accept this socially constructed narrative as fact, because there are

birth certificates with these binary designations and institutions that were created to legitimize them, shaming anyone who dares to exist outside of this narrative.

While a lot of people like myself are privileged to identify with the gender they were assigned at birth, unsurprisingly, a lot of people do not. It doesn't mean there's anything wrong with them. As described by activist and spoken-word poet Alok Vaid-Menon, "I wasn't born in the wrong body. I was born in the wrong world." A world that predetermines every detail of your life and how it will look, right down to the color of your clothing. And this is before you've even exited the womb, based on the way your genitals formed in utero. Bonkers, right?

Gender is entirely different from sex. "Sex" typically refers to genitalia—the biological differences between "male" and "female" bodies. Your gender is how you choose to identify, your perception of yourself, and how you feel you identify within our society's ideas of gender. If you don't feel you identify with male or female, you might choose to adopt the label "nonbinary" or "gender-fluid" and use gender-neutral pronouns such as they/them. Gender is not a fixed, half-pink, half-blue, two-dimensional shape. Just like sexuality, it exists on a glorious multidimensional spectrum and cannot be assumed based on someone's genitals or how they dress.

Gender expression, gender identity, and sexuality are not intrinsically linked.

I identify as a woman, the gender I was assigned at birth. So I am a cisgender woman. This is my *gender identity.*

The way I dress, how I do my hair and makeup, and present my gender is my *gender expression.*

I date people of all genders, I identify as queer, and this is my *sexuality.* None of these affects the others.

However, my *sexuality* is constantly assumed to be straight because my *gender expression* is very feminine, and by default, we assume that femininity is performed exclusively for men.

If people stopped assuming that I was straight and instead had an open mind, it might mean that I wouldn't have to constantly come out to people— every single day.

Just because a cisgender man wears a pink dress, it does not automatically mean that he's transgender or that he's gay. He's just a man who likes to wear pink dresses. Colors don't have a gender. Clothes merely communicate connotations and assumptions about socially constructed ideas of gender.

No matter how liberal your household was when you were growing up, it's impossible to escape the gender binary and heteronormative ways of thinking. They have penetrated every facet of our lives. But there are ways that we can consciously rewrite this narrative and reduce the impact it has on our lives and the lives of people who come after us. We can start with our language. Using gender-neutral pronouns like "they" and "them" when we're not sure of someone's preferred pronouns shows consideration. It shows that we haven't *assumed*.

FEMALE ARTIST

There are certain harmful "defaults" in our society: whiteness, binary gender, and heterosexuality. I am constantly referred to as a "female artist" or "female illustrator," and my friends who are in bands are referred to as "female musicians." At first glance, this may not seem offensive. But words hold so much power, and what adding "female"

WE CAN'T FORCE A ONE-SIZE-FITS-ALL NARRATIVE ON BILLIONS OF PEOPLE AND EXPECT IT TO FIT EVERY SINGLE ONE OF THEM.

TRANS PEOPLE **EXIST;** DEAL WITH IT.

JUST BECAUSE
WE CAN EXPLAIN
SOMEONE'S
BEHAVIOR,
THAT DOES NOT MEAN
WE EXCUSE IT.

as a descriptor implies is that artists, musicians, and illustrators are inherently male. You would never hear anyone say "male artist." The same default bias is highlighted in the predictable backlash when a book character assumed to be white is portrayed by a person of color in a film or TV adaptation. Whiteness is so default that only recently were there ballet shoes and flesh-colored bandages produced in varying skin tones. My landlord told me someone was coming over to check the gas, and I was (pleasantly) surprised when a woman showed up at my door. When you come across yourself assuming these defaults, try to catch yourself in that moment and remember that these stereotypes are a powerful tool of oppression, because they are used to keep marginalized and oppressed people "in their place."

MIND YOUR BIAS
All of us have bias filters and they vary, depending on our upbringing, experiences, and the narratives we absorb about ourselves and others in the media. We mostly operate from the subconscious part of our minds, and the stereotypes we've absorbed can impact our behavior without us even realizing it, resulting in microaggressions.

Here are some microaggressions you might be guilty of:
- Crossing the street or clutching your purse tighter when you see a Black man.
- Asking people of color, "But where are you really from?"
- Asking gay couples, "Which one's the man, and which one's the woman?"
- White women saying, "Hey guuuurl," and snapping their fingers at their Black girlfriends, when they would never do this with their white counterparts.
- Telling a person of color they are "articulate."

- Using disablist slurs such as "ret*rd" or "crazy."
- Asking a woman about her "boyfriend/husband" when she has only ever referred to a "partner."
- "She's trans? Wow, I would have had no idea—she looks like a real woman."
- Trying to set up a gay person you meet with "your other gay friend."
- Saying that Black hair is "unprofessional," asking questions about Black hair, vocalizing opinions on Black hair, or asking to touch Black hair.
- Men interrupting women when they're talking in meetings with, "Well, actually, I think . . ."
- Asking women what they were wearing when they recount experiences of sexual harassment or assault.
- Calling women of color "exotic."
- Men saying, "You're not like other girls" (or women saying, "I'm not like other girls").
- Hosting panel discussions, events, and exhibitions with all-white or all-male participants, artists, or speakers.
- Calling neighborhoods "sketchy" when they just predominantly consist of Black and minority ethnic people.
- Singing the N-word in songs (you'd think us non-Black folks would have caught on to this by now, but I'm putting it here, just in case).

The difference between microaggressions like these and overt racism/sexism/homophobia is that microaggressions are unintentional. We don't know in our conscious mind that we are "othering" this person based on our subconscious beliefs about them, which were formed from years of socialization.

While this explains our behavior, it does not *excuse* it. When people call us out on these behaviors, our priority should always be to make sure that the person we've hurt is okay. Whether you intended to hurt them or not, the truth is that you did. The impact of our actions is always more important than our intentions if we have caused someone harm. The next chapter focuses on accountability and apologizing.

So. Listen to people who have experiences outside of your own and be mindful of how you treat them, stop assuming people's sexuality, and always ask for someone's pronouns if you're unsure.

Got it?

CHAPTER 19

ACCOUNTABILITY

When the people in your life call you out on your behavior or hold you accountable for your actions, it is an act of love.

It might feel like a personal attack initially, but if someone cares enough to tell you that something you have said is hurtful or has hurt them, it's because they value you and they want you to understand how your words affected them. Equally, holding yourself accountable for your own actions is self-love. This is how we grow.

If you're going to leave room for growth and to form meaningful connections in your life, it's necessary to get over your need to be right all the time.

Phrases to avoid when apologizing:
-   "I'm sorry you feel this way, but . . ."
-   "I think you've taken this the wrong way."
-   "I think you're overreacting."
-   "I didn't mean it like that."
-   "I don't think that's fair because . . ."

Those are reactions. Not responses.

A response is carefully formulated after you have processed what has been said and have had time to empathize with the perspective offered up to you. A response includes self-reflection; it involves you looking inward.

It doesn't matter what you meant or what your intentions were. What matters is the impact of your actions and that they have harmed someone. Someone is hurt! Your priority should be rectifying the situation and reducing the damage to make this person feel as safe as possible. The best lesson I ever learned was to work on getting out of the habit of reacting, and start responding instead. When someone calls you out on your behavior, your initial reaction might be to defend yourself, because you can't for a second imagine that you are capable of hurting someone, especially if it was unintentional.

But if someone is hurt, they want an apology—not an excuse.

Sure, if you feel it's necessary, you can explain your side of things, but verbally acknowledge that, while this explains your behavior, it does not excuse it. It does not excuse that someone is hurt.

HOW TO RESPOND

Let's work through a hypothetical. Say your friend has confronted you about how they feel you've been ignoring them lately. They say that you've been spending a lot of time with your new partner, that they're delighted for you because your happiness means everything to them, but your new relationship has made them feel shut out. How should you process this and make sure you're responding rather than reacting?

Apologize

It doesn't matter that you didn't mean to make them feel that way; the fact is that they do feel that way, and their feelings are valid. Tell

LEARN HOW TO ADMIT WHEN YOU'RE WRONG. APOLOGIZE WITHOUT EXCUSES AND VIEW MISTAKES AS OPPORTUNITIES FOR GROWTH.

them this. Let them know that you have acknowledged their feelings and that you are sorry.

"I'm so sorry I have caused you to feel this way—you didn't deserve to feel like that."

"Your feelings are entirely valid."

"Thank you for sharing this with me."

You might feel angry

Your initial defense response might be that you think they're "jealous"—but if you feel angry or you feel the need to defend and excuse why you did what you did, stop right there. The best thing to do in this situation is to give yourself time to cool down and self-reflect. When we become defensive, we put ourselves at the center of the situation—and this isn't about you; it's about your friend and making sure they feel safe and comfortable enough to talk to you about their feelings. When we become defensive and say things like "You're overreacting!" or "You're just jealous," we cause the person to doubt their feelings and foster a hostile environment. It's a form of emotional gaslighting. This person won't feel comfortable vocalizing their feelings to you again, and if this cycle repeats itself enough times, it forms the foundation of an emotionally abusive relationship. If someone feels they can't speak up in a relationship, it's abusive.

Acknowledge that you may have overlooked their needs

You might have prioritized your new relationship over your friendship. That even though this wasn't your intention, you acknowledge this has made them feel upset, and you want to come to a solution. Ask what this means for them and what actions they feel are necessary to rectify the situation. Or if you can think of something, suggest it yourself! There's nothing better than having your feelings acknowledged by someone who also proactively tries to find a solution to make you feel better. Be actively engaged in reaching a solution.

Come back with correct behavior

Apologies without changed behavior are insincere since you are not seeking to resolve what has gone wrong. What can you do moving forward to make sure that you don't encounter this situation again?

Having a conversation like this requires both people to put aside their egos and talk directly to one another to find a solution. If this kind of straightforward communication is hard for you, try writing an email or a text instead. Direct and face-to-face conversations can be overwhelming for people who struggle with anxiety and other mental illnesses, but there are always other ways to take accountability and resolve conflict that don't require this level of stress. I find that texts and emails work better for me personally, usually followed up with a phone call to get more of a back and forth about how we can find a solution. It can be hard to understand someone's tone through text, leading to further miscommunication. So building a conversation can be a useful and effective means to a quicker and more sustainable resolution.

HOLDING SOMEONE ELSE ACCOUNTABLE

Setting and holding boundaries is a way to filter out the people who don't deserve to be in your life. How a person responds to my boundaries, or how they respond to me telling them that they have done something hurtful, helps me decide whether or not I should keep them around.

If someone can't put aside their ego to consider someone else's perspective, realize that they exist outside of their own perception, and

IF PEOPLE CAN'T
BE ACCOUNTABLE
OR APOLOGIZE
FOR HURTING SOMEONE
—WHETHER THEY
MEANT TO OR NOT—
IT'S A RED FLAG.
NO,
IT'S <u>THE</u> RED FLAG.

that *gasp* they are, in fact, human and they made a mistake, they are not the kind of person you want in your life. Compromise? *For what!* Why should I change my boundaries when the reason they're there in the first place is to protect me from things that I know from experience will cause me harm?

Red-flag responses when you try to hold someone accountable:
- You feel the need to back down from your initial statement or change it to make it more palatable because they got defensive.
- Their reaction makes you feel the need to apologize for not "saying it nicely." Remember, they're the person who owes an apology.
- You feel as though you are walking on eggshells because you're worried about how they might react.
- They say they "don't feel like they have anything to apologize for."
- They go to great lengths to explain why they did what they did, their thought process behind it, and so on, instead of just acknowledging that you're hurt and that they're responsible.
- They turn themselves into the victim and start talking about what they're going through.
- They try to shame you by making you feel "too much" for setting your boundary.
- They refuse to apologize.

Equally, if you have ever exhibited any of these behaviors yourself, now is a good time to reflect and examine why these feelings came up for you and why you felt the need to defend yourself in this way. It's okay; we all fuck up. But you might owe someone an apology.

If someone becomes defensive, tells me I could have expressed my hurt "a different way," or refuses to say sorry because they "haven't done anything wrong"—they will not be hearing from me again. At least, not until they recognize what they have done. Even then, you do not owe anyone your forgiveness.

You will never receive an apology from someone who refuses to see your perspective because they will always believe that they've done nothing wrong.

Forget it.

You tried.

Move on.

Focus on your healing.

Their karma is being who they are.

CHAPTER 20

CHECK YOUR PRIVILEGE

What does privilege really mean?

To have privilege is to be afforded unearned benefits in society based on being part of a social group.

It's possible to be both oppressed and privileged at the same time. For example, I'm a queer woman and face oppression from homophobia and sexism, but I am also extremely privileged in that I am white, thin, nondisabled, cisgender, and neurotypical, so I am afforded more opportunities at the expense of people who don't have these privileges.

We are far more likely to be aware of our negative experiences of oppression rather than the ways in which we are privileged. We assume how we're treated is how everyone else is treated, because it's our reality and it feels "normal." Privilege is invisible to the person who has it until it's pointed out to them or until after they have lost that privilege. For example, I didn't realize what a privilege it was to be able to show public displays of affection until I began dating women and I began to fear for our safety from just holding hands in public.

178

The thing about privilege is that it can't exist without oppression. The reason you are privileged is because another group is suffering and paying for it. Ever wondered why people cause such a fuss over white girls in cornrows and braids? Because the act of being able to "dip into" Black culture and not face the struggles that they do when they perform their own culture is rooted in an unspeakable amount of privilege. Black women are told their hair is "ghetto" in cornrows and "unprofessional" when they wear it natural, and Black kids are sent home from school because their natural hair is "too distracting." It's a privilege to be able to adopt parts of Black culture as a person who benefits from their oppression. Exercising our privilege in this way is harmful and offensive, and until Black people can live their lives without being punished for their hair, white people in dreadlocks will never be "just a hairstyle." It will always be political.

Scholar and activist Peggy McIntosh describes white privilege as "an invisible package of unearned assets that I can count on cashing in each day, but about which I was 'meant' to remain oblivious. White privilege is like an invisible weightless knapsack of special provisions, maps, passports, codebooks, visas, clothes, tools, and blank checks."

A white person can be oppressed for a number of reasons, but never because they're white. Having privilege does not mean that you haven't had a hard life or worked hard to get to where you are. It just means that someone else in your position without your privileges would face a lot more obstacles to get there. For example, a white person living in poverty still has white privilege, because being Black and poor is harder. We have multiple components to our identities, and we are able to be both oppressed and privileged in different ways at the same time. For example, white women in power are still capable of holding up

racism-based systems, and men of color are capable of perpetuating and maintaining patriarchy.

Here are some privilege checklists to help you recognize where you might have been given a leg up in society.[3]

White race, ethnicity, and culture privilege

❑ People know how to pronounce my name.

❑ I am never mocked or perceived as a threat because of my name.

❑ I don't feel threatened by police.

❑ People of my race are widely represented in media.

❑ I don't ever have to think about my race or ethnicity.

❑ I don't really think about race at all.

❑ I do not have to worry about imprisonment unless I commit a serious crime.

❑ Products in a "nude" color more or less match my skin.

❑ My ethnicity will not make people around me uncomfortable.

❑ I can shop knowing that no one will be suspicious of me.

❑ I don't have to check whether my ethnicity will cause problems when choosing travel destinations.

---

3   Boise State Writing Center, https://sites.google.com/a/u.boisestate.edu/social-justice-training/about-us/our-training/privilege-checklist

Cisgender privilege

❑ I can use public facilities like restrooms and locker rooms without fear of verbal abuse, assault, or arrest.

❑ People can generally assume what to call me and how to refer to me without asking first.

❑ I do not have to worry that my gender expression will make people around me uncomfortable.

❑ Strangers don't ask me what my genitals look like or how I have sex.

❑ I have the ability to walk through the world and blend in because of my gender expression.

❑ If I end up in the emergency room, I do not have to worry that my gender will keep me from receiving appropriate treatment or that all of my medical issues will be seen as a result of my gender.

❑ I am able to purchase clothes that I like without being refused service/mocked by staff or questioned about my gender.

❑ My gender is an option on all forms I may have to complete.

❑ I am legally recognized as a gender.

❑ I don't have to worry about being fetishized to satisfy a curiosity or kink pertaining to my gender identity.

Male/male passing privilege

- ❏ I can express myself, set boundaries, and be assertive without being called a "bitch."

- ❏ I am perceived as an individual and my actions are not seen as reflective of my entire gender.

- ❏ I can walk the streets and enter public spaces without the threat of sexual harassment.

- ❏ At work, I don't often have to worry about harassment from customers, coworkers, or bosses.

- ❏ I generally feel comfortable going somewhere alone at whatever time.

- ❏ I feel comfortable going on a date with someone new, as I don't have to fear violence (pertains to straight men).

- ❏ I don't have to worry about people perceiving me as sexual because of my clothes or body.

- ❏ People do not often make unsolicited comments about my body.

- ❏ I am not expected to spend a great deal of time and money on my appearance or shamed if I don't.

- ❏ I do not often have to fear sexual violence.

- ❏ When I speak up, my opinions are heard and respected equally with other people's.

- ❏ I am not diminished or treated differently because of my gender.

PRIVILEGE IS USUALLY INVISIBLE TO THE PERSON WHO HAS IT UNTIL IT'S POINTED OUT TO THEM, OR UNTIL THEY HAVE LOST THAT PRIVILEGE.

Straight privilege

❏   I will receive public recognition/support for a romantic relationship.

❏   I feel comfortable displaying affection in public with my partner and don't expect hostile or violent reactions from others.

❏   I don't have to check that my sexuality is legal when choosing travel destinations with my partner.

❏   I can openly live with my partner.

❏   I have never had to hide or reveal my sexuality.

❏   I have never experienced discrimination at work for my sexuality.

❏   I can see my sexuality and type of relationships represented in movies and television.

❏   I have access to role models of my sexual orientation with whom I can identify.

❏   I can assume I am around others of my sexuality most of the time and don't have to worry about being the only person of my sexuality in a class, job, or social situation.

❏   I can talk about my relationship without fearing judgment or violence.

❏   I can easily live in a neighborhood in which people will accept me.

❏   If I raise, adopt, or teach children, no one will assume that I will somehow force them into my sexuality.

❏   Strangers don't ask me how I have sex or how I could have children.

❏   I will not be mistreated by the police or people in authority because of my sexuality.

Nondisabled privilege

❑ I can go to new places knowing that I will be able to move through the space with ease and without preplanning.

❑ I do not have to worry about making the people around me uncomfortable because of my disability.

❑ People treat me like an adult—they do not crouch down to me, use a patronizing tone, or offer unsolicited help for tasks.

❑ I can succeed in situations without other people being surprised by that success or using the word "despite."

❑ My success is not presented as a guilt trip for others who do not have my disability. ("If they can do it despite their disability, what's your excuse?")

❑ I can go to any class, job, or website and assume that the materials presented to me will be understandable.

❑ People don't think I'm lazy or stupid when I need to try something again or ask something to be made clearer.

❑ I am able to enter new situations without fear of debilitating anxiety, embarrassment, harassment, or violence.

❑ No one assumes that any partner attracted to me must be a predator or pedophile, even though I am an adult.

Class/financial privilege

❑ I have usually had access to health care.

❑ I have access to transportation that will get me where I need to go.

❑ I have knowledge of and access to community resources.

❑ I can swear or commit a crime without people attributing it to the low morals of my class.

❑ I can update my wardrobe with new clothes to match current styles and trends.

❑ People do not assume that I am unintelligent or lazy based on the dialect I grew up speaking.

❑ I live in a safe environment, with access to heating, cooling, and clean water.

❑ I know that I will be able to go to a well stocked grocery store when I need to and will be able to buy what I want.

❑ Whenever I've moved out of my home it has been voluntary and I had another home to move into.

❑ I can plan on getting a raise at my job.

❑ My decision to go or not to go to college wasn't based entirely on financial considerations.

Privilege works in systems and institutions of power. People with institutional power—the executives of large corporations and media companies (there are more CEOs of S&P 1500 companies named John than there are female CEOs altogether), politicians, and pundits—can use their positions to benefit themselves and other privileged people like them. If you are oppressed, you do not have this institutional power because your race/class/gender is simply not represented enough in these institutions. Black people do not have racial institutional power; women do not have gender-based institutional power. Therefore, "reverse racism" and "female privilege" do not exist because, in order to cause oppression, you need the backing of institutional power behind you. Misandry (the hatred of men) has never led to widespread career limitations, rape, murder, or mass oppression for men the way that misogyny (the hatred of women) has for women.

We must look at the rule and not the exceptions to the rule. People will point to specific successful individuals like Oprah Winfrey or Barack Obama to prove that "racism is over," but privilege and oppression work as a toxic system that perpetuates itself. Let's say a company is full of white cisgender men. They claim that they hire based on "qualifications" and that they "don't discriminate." But even if this were so and only the most academically qualified applicants were hired, in our society, people of color are less likely to have been able to achieve the same educational qualifications as their white counterparts. The socioeconomic reality of being part of an oppressed group often means they don't have access to the same quality of education as those with racial and class privilege. They're more likely to grow up in poorer areas with lower-quality schools; universities are less likely to accept minority students because of racial bias; and even when they are accepted, they are less likely to graduate because of lack of support in their studies. So the company hires only the "most qualified," but qualifications are not equitably accessible, resulting in de facto discrimination. And this dynamic permeates all facets of our lives—from education and career opportunities to housing and health care.

Read that shit again.

All of the little microaggressions and instances of racism that filter through our society are what keeps the cycle of oppression in motion, maintaining a status quo that keeps privileged people at the top.

It's crucial that we are aware of how nothing in our lives is untouched by our privilege. The point of being cognizant of our privileges is not to engender feelings of guilt—guilt without action is pointless and does nothing for social change.

But being aware of our privilege allows us to use it to benefit other people. As we move through the world, we must think of the opportunities we could give or how we could make way for people who don't have the same access to important spaces that we do.

Are you hiring people for a new project? Make sure that there are people of color on board. Have you been asked to speak on an all-white panel? Decline the invite, tell them why, and suggest they present a greater diversity of perspectives. Have you seen a woman or a visibly queer person being harassed on the street? Walk with them, make sure they feel safe, and intervene if you can. The only way to break these cycles and create a world where people are treated equally is to challenge these systems *and ourselves.*

CHAPTER 21

LET THAT SHIT GO

TRIGGER WARNING: THEMES OF SEXUAL TRAUMA

There will never be a point in your life when you're entirely "healed." But whether it's a breakup or something more traumatic— shit gets better.

There are parts of myself that I have lost to traumatic events, and I'm not sure if I will ever get them back. Accepting that I will never be the same despite how unfair these events have been has helped me to move through them, rather than be destroyed by them. I learned the important and hard truth that my healing process is my responsibility and no one else's. The same way you cannot fix other people, no one else can heal and fix you. There's no need to find a "lesson" in your experience or to try to be the same person you were before it happened. Finding meaning in traumatic events should not be your priority; your priority should be trying to survive. I hate the phrase "everything happens for a reason" when used in the context of trauma, because terrible things happen all the time, to good people and bad, for no reason at all. If your healing process is contingent on validation from other people or an apology, you will never be free of the control it exerts over you. Accepting this fact alone played an enormous part in the healing process that I'm still working through every single day.

ARE YOU HEALED OR ARE YOU JUST DISTRACTED?
- @werenotreallystrangers

In the past, I have utilized little coping mechanisms and pockets of joy that temporarily felt like glue, filling up the cracks caused by trauma and helping to make me feel whole again. This could be dating someone new, having a casual fling, ordering myself takeout, or spending money on skincare products to make myself feel better. But using things that afford us only temporary, transient relief for a much deeper and complex problem—reaching for the quick-fix coping mechanisms—never fully heals us. We cannot rely on instant solutions or insubstantial "glue" to fill our wounds; we must instead allow them to heal properly on their own, forming stronger, lasting bonds through self-reflection, accountability, and community. We cannot heal by using external factors and validation. It has to come from within.

The thing about short-term gratification, however beautiful and effective it feels in the moment, is that it is fleeting. If left unchecked, it often results in self-destructive behaviors, which end up prolonging our suffering, making us weaker and less able to take care of ourselves. Self-sabotage could be anything from binge drinking or eating to checking up religiously on your ex's Instagram account to compulsive purchases. You might not even realize you're doing it, but all are acts of self-sabotage detrimental to long-term healing. To say "I'm healed" isn't the goal—the goal is to get out of the place in your head where you are an obstacle to your own progress.

Finding the power to say "no" to things, people, and habits that impede my journey back to finding myself has been my single most important act of self-care. In a world that encourages selflessness in women and in which we are expected to be caregivers and nurturers, we often neglect ourselves in the process. Self-neglect is best healed through deep introspection. It involves discomfort. It involves being willing to admit that everything you thought you knew about the world, other people, and yourself may be fictions you told yourself in order to cope and stay in a comfortable, familiar state of suffering. These are called "limiting narratives"; they are the stories we tell ourselves over and over again to justify why things might not be working out for us in life. The only way to escape this cyclical, insufferable hell is to examine our behaviors and ask ourselves what needs to change.

You can only become a more refined version of your already incredible self if you question everything.

"YOU'VE CHANGED!"

Outgrowing other people as well as habits is part of the healing and growth process. If you want to grow, you're going to have to ditch what holds you back. The only person in control of your happiness is you—make changes if you need to. Toxic people hate to see you get out of situations that kept you grounded and suffering like they are—it reminds them of their own lack of growth, especially if you've bonded with this person over a shared trauma. Trauma-bonding with people is very real, and it's another subtle way of self-sabotaging your growth. You might cling to those who share a similar trauma or hang around with people who remind you of the

version of yourself that existed before the trauma happened. You cannot grow in these relationships, because your entire connection is built on mutual suffering.

When you're growing and have decided to implement boundaries in your life, you may hear things like:

- "You think you're so much better than everyone now."
- "You've changed!"
- "Sorry I'm not good enough for you anymore."
- "You used to be fun."
- "Everything's about boundaries—loosen up."

All of these are forms of emotional manipulation. There are people in the world who are aching to see you thrive and get out of your cycle of self-sabotage. Outgrowing people who do not support your growth is an act of choosing your own happiness and makes room for people who deserve a place in your life. *Let that shit go.*

HOW I GOT TO KNOW MYSELF, FALL IN LOVE WITH MYSELF, AND HEAL MYSELF

At its core, nurturing self-love can be ugly. It's not always face masks and selfies. For me, it involved a lot of crying, isolation, setting boundaries, and self-reflection. Self-care looks different for everyone, but here's how I shed the shrunken version of myself that I had become, with the steps I took to grow into my new, divine self:

- I cried my eyes out while sitting on the floor talking to myself in the mirror.
- I took myself out for lunch, on my own.
- I got myself into therapy.
- I grew out all of my body hair.
- I kept a handwritten diary recording how I felt on a day-to-day basis.
- I danced naked around my apartment to my favorite music, free of any kind of gaze but my own.
- I invested in my health and self-healing.
- I bought and read books.
- I bought my first vibrator to reclaim my body (and give myself earth-shattering orgasms, of course).
- I stopped isolating myself by telling my friends how I'd been feeling for the first time.
- I talked to and hyped myself up in the mirror on a daily basis.
- I recorded videos talking to the camera for when I'm feeling low, as a cathartic release and to recognize my self-destructive patterns.
- I cried and screamed into my pillow.
- I took hundreds of nudes that to this day no one else has seen but me.
- I hung gorgeous art in my home to surround myself with visually stimulating things I love.
- I shouted "FUCK YOU" to get myself out of bed in the mornings when it was hard, as a way of giving up the power that trauma had over me and my daily routine.
- I bought houseplants to look after, tend to, and water daily. (On days when you feel undeserving, like the world doesn't need you, your plants still do.)
- I cried on FaceTime to friends for hours.
- I bought cute lingerie to look good for my own goddamn self.

- I started to say "NO" instead of worrying about people's reactions and stuck to my decisions; I decided to stop people-pleasing and put up some boundaries.
- I overcame my FOMO and stayed at home.
- I avoided situations, events, or people that would impact the progress I had been making to heal myself.

Some things do develop beyond discomfort and turn into diagnosable mental health problems, such as depression, PTSD, and eating disorders. At this point, simple self-care and self-reflection aren't enough, and external care is required. For this reason exactly, I go to therapy weekly! If you do need help, and you feel it's safe to, you should confide in your friends or family.

FOR PERSPECTIVE

Healing is hard. If you have a tricky time appreciating the journey you've been on and how incredible it is that you're alive, I want you to imagine all the past versions of yourself, standing right in front of you. This could be:

- The person who was bullied in high school.
- The person who cried themselves to sleep.
- The one who drunk-sobbed in the bathroom on a night out.
- The one who went through something so traumatic they thought their life was broken beyond repair.
- The one who almost gave up on life completely.

Imagine all of the past versions of yourself, standing right in front of you. They are all smiling, looking back at you. They are so proud of you.

Because you beat what they were going through. You beat the things that tried to kill and destroy them. Because of your strength, you are still here in this present moment, in spite of what happened to those past versions of yourself.

They are grateful because you got all of them through this to be where you are today—alive.

GLOSSARY

Accountability – taking responsibility for your actions, words, and beliefs. Being accountable ensures that people are answerable for the things they do, especially those things that could cause harm.

Ageism – discriminating against somebody on the basis of their age. This can affect both older and younger people, who might not be taken seriously because of their age, who are told they should or should not act in a certain way because of their age, or who are treated badly because they are perceived to be too young or too old.

Butch – a person who is butch is somebody who has traits that are stereotypically described as masculine. Although often used within the lesbian community, not all butch women are lesbians (and not all lesbians are butch).

Capitalism – an exploitative economic system focused on creating profit. Businesses, properties, and industry are owned privately (as opposed to by the state or collectively by workers) and are designed to create profit for those who own them.

Cisgender – a person who is the gender that they were assigned at birth. If a person was described as a girl when they were born, and still identify as a girl later in life, they are cisgender. Essentially, it means "not trans."

Fatphobia – prejudice or discrimination against somebody because they are fat. This can include not providing suitable accommodations (e.g., only having narrow chairs with arms), judging somebody for how their body looks in clothes ("She can't get away with a miniskirt!"), or not hiring somebody because of stereotypical judgments about their weight.

Femme – a person whose identity or gender presentation tends towards being feminine can be described as femme. In the trans community, people can describe themselves as femme without identifying as a woman; it is a distinct identity that leans towards the feminine.

Heteronormative – a state in which heterosexuality is considered to be the norm and other sexual orientations are marginalized. A heteronormative movie might only have heterosexual relationships, for example.

Internalized misogyny – a state in which women turn the hatred of women (misogyny) against themselves and other women, and believe and perpetuate negative gender stereotypes.

Intersectional feminism – the acknowledgment of how oppression based on aspects of one's identity overlaps to create unique experiences of discrimination. Originally coined by Kimberlé Williams Crenshaw.

LGBTQ+ – a range of sexualities and gender identities that vary from heteronormative to cisnormative ones. LGBTQ stands for lesbian, gay, bisexual, transgender, and queer, and the + indicates that more exist, such as intersex, aromantic, asexual, questioning, etc.

Male gaze – the hegemonic perspective of cisgender, heterosexual men present in art, media, and culture, which everyone internalizes to an extent.

Marginalized – a marginalized group is one that is discriminated against due to an inherent characteristic. Nonwhite people, disabled people, fat people, women, working-class people, and older/younger people can all be marginalized in various ways.

#MeToo – a movement started by Tarana Burke, where people have opened up about the sexual harassment they have experienced at the hands of men.

Misogyny – prejudice or discrimination against women, often expressed as hatred, dismissal, or contempt.

Nondisabled – people who are not disabled are nondisabled. This term is preferred because the alternative, "able-bodied," could include people